150 Recipes series

150

STIR-FRY
recipes

....

INSPIRED IDEAS FOR
EVERYDAY COOKING

CONTENTS

INTRODUCTION

For a simple, speedy mid-week supper or lunch, a sizzling stir-fry is hard to beat. Stir-frying is an ever popular, quick method of cooking and typically everything is cooked together in one pan, so it's easy to rustle-up tasty, nutritious and hassle-free meals.

With this inspiring selection of sensational stir-fries, which includes amazing appetizers and side dishes, plus a multitude of magnificent main course dishes, you can discover the wonder of the wok and create some marvellous meals, many in just a matter of minutes.

You'll find flavour-packed dishes from across the globe to suit all palates and occasions, many of which are sure to earn a regular slot at your table. It's immensely satisfying to stir-fry, so prepare to perfect your skills, cook with

confidence and create some fantastic stir-fries for family and friends.

We start with an inspiring collection of appealing appetizers and tempting side dishes, ideal for sharing with friends. Choose from classics such as Egg-fried Rice, Sweet & Sour Spare Ribs and Chicken Noodle Soup, or try something else like Tempura Vegetables or Pork Meatballs in Lemon Grass & Chilli Broth with Pak Choi.

A chapter of mouth-watering meat-based stir-fries encompasses simple suppers such as Sweet & Sour Pork, Hot Sesame Beef and Lamb with Black Bean Sauce, as well as choice creations like Spicy Sichuan Pork, Ginger Beef with Yellow Peppers and Stir-fried Lamb with Orange.

Next on the menu is a tempting selection of poultry-based stir-fries, perfect for fuss-free family meals. Popular chicken classics include Chicken Chow Mein, Chicken Fried Rice and Sweet & Sour Chicken, while turkey and duck are featured in superb stir-fries such as Paprika Turkey Strips, Turkey Teriyaki and Fruity Duck Stir-fry.

Fabulous fish and seafood stir-fries follow, providing tempting weeknight pleasers like Caramelized Tuna Salad, Simple Stir-fried Scallops and Thai

Prawn Noodle Bowl. Or tempt guests to the table with Five-willow Fish, Salt and Pepper Squid with Ginger Wisps or Spicy Seafood Stew, all certain to deliver on flavour.

Finally, for some inspiring meat-free meals, make the most of vegetables with the super section on vegetable based stir-fries, featuring some delicious dishes including Sweet & Sour Tofu with Vegetables, Stir-fried Butternut Squash and Thai Noodle Salad.

A wok is best for cooking stir-fries, and although a heavy-based frying pan can successfully be used, a wok is the ideal utensil. Woks are usually made from stainless steel or cast iron and are readily obtainable in various diameters; non-stick woks are also available. Their unique rounded-bottom shape with curved sides allows food to be continuously stirred and tossed during cooking using a wooden spatula, wooden spoon or chopsticks. Woks can also be used for deep-frying. Some come with a trivet/rack and domed lid, ideal for steaming vegetables, fish steaks and chicken breasts; others come with a bamboo steamer basket. A new cast iron wok will need 'seasoning' before use to prevent rusting and stop food sticking during cooking (follow the manufacturer's guidelines on how to season your wok).

Stir-frying is typically done over a high heat, so the food cooks quickly and evenly, retaining much of its colour and goodness. The amount of oil used in many stir-fries is minimal so generally it's a healthy cooking method too.

Prepare all the ingredients in advance, cutting them into similar-sized pieces to ensure even cooking. Measure out other ingredients like oil, sauces and seasonings before you begin cooking.

The wok is usually preheated before oil is added, then the oil is heated until hot and sizzling, before the food is added. The prepared ingredients are added to the wok in stages during cooking, adding those that need longer cooking first, followed by those that require less cooking.

APPETIZERS & SIDE DISHES

EGG-FRIED RICE

Serves: 4   **Prep: 5 mins**   **Cook: 7 mins**

Ingredients

2 tbsp vegetable or groundnut oil

350 g/12 oz cooked rice

1 egg, well beaten

salt and pepper

Method

1 Heat a wok over a medium heat, then add the oil. Add the rice and stir-fry for 1 minute.

2 Using a fork, break down the rice as much as possible into individual grains.

3 Quickly add the egg, stirring to coat each piece of rice.

4 Continue to stir until the egg is cooked and the rice, as far as possible, is in single grains. Season with salt and pepper. Check that the rice is piping hot before serving.

★ Variation

For extra colour and texture, stir in some fried flaked almonds and chopped chives.

PRAWN TOASTS

Makes: 16   **Prep: 20 mins**   **Cook: 15 mins**

Ingredients

100 g/3½ oz raw prawns,
peeled and deveined

2 egg whites,
kept separate

2 tbsp cornflour

½ tsp sugar

pinch of salt

2 tbsp finely chopped fresh
coriander leaves

2 slices day-old white bread

vegetable or groundnut oil,
for deep-frying

Method

1 Pound the prawns to a pulp with a pestle and mortar.

2 Mix the prawns with one of the egg whites and 1 tablespoon of the cornflour. Add the sugar and salt and stir in the coriander. Mix the remaining egg white with the remaining cornflour.

3 Remove the crusts from the bread and cut each slice into 8 triangles. Brush the top of each piece with the egg white and cornflour mixture, then add 1 teaspoon of the prawn mixture. Smooth the top.

4 Heat enough oil for deep-frying in a wok, until it reaches 180–190°C/350–375°F, or until a cube of bread browns in 30 seconds. Fry the toasts prawn-side down for about 2 minutes. Turn and fry for a further 2 minutes until golden.

5 Remove the prawn toasts with a slotted spoon, drain on kitchen paper and serve warm.

DEEP-FRIED VEGETABLE SPRING ROLLS

Makes: 10

Prep: 20–25 mins, plus marinating & cooling

Cook: 25 mins

Ingredients

10 spring roll wrappers,
16 cm/6¼ inches diameter,
thawed if frozen

1 egg white, lightly beaten

groundnut oil,
for deep-frying

sweet chilli dipping sauce,
to serve

Marinade

1-cm/½-inch piece fresh
ginger

½ tbsp sweet chilli sauce

1 tbsp soy sauce

Filling

115 g/4 oz firm tofu

2 tbsp groundnut oil,
plus extra for greasing

1 carrot, halved lengthways
and sliced into thin
semi-circles

1 green chilli, deseeded
and finely chopped

3 spring onions,
finely chopped

2 garlic cloves,
finely chopped

55 g/2 oz shiitake
mushrooms, tough stalks
discarded, finely chopped

50 g/1¾ oz mung
beansprouts

salt and pepper

Method

1 Cut the tofu into small cubes. To make the marinade, squeeze the ginger in a garlic press, combine the remaining marinade ingredients and pour over the tofu. Leave to marinate for 30 minutes.

2 To make the filling, preheat a wok over a high heat. Add the oil and heat until very hot. Add the carrot and stir-fry over a medium–high heat for 1 minute. Add the chilli, spring onions and garlic. Stir-fry for 30 seconds, then add the mushrooms. Stir-fry for a further 1 minute. Add the beansprouts and season to taste with salt and pepper. Add the tofu and the marinade, and stir-fry for a further 2 minutes. Tip the filling into a bowl and leave to cool.

3 Place a heaped tablespoon of filling across the lower third of a spring roll wrapper, leaving a 3-cm/1¼-inch margin on either side. Fold the bottom edge over the filling, then roll once to secure. Fold in the sides, sealing with egg white. Continue rolling to make a neat cylindrical package about 10 cm/4 inches wide. Seal with egg white.

4 Continue until all the wrappers are filled, placing them on a lightly greased plate.

APPETIZERS & SIDE DISHES

5 Heat enough oil for deep-frying in a large wok until it reaches 180–190°C/350–375°F, or until a cube of bread browns in 30 seconds.

6 Add a few rolls at a time to the wok, without overcrowding, and deep-fry for about 4 minutes, turning occasionally, until pale golden in colour. Remove with a slotted spoon and drain on kitchen paper.

7 Reheat the oil to 180°C/350°F, then return the rolls to the oil and deep-fry for 1–2 minutes, until golden and crisp. Drain and serve immediately with the sweet chilli dipping sauce.

BEEF FRIED RICE

Serves: 6   **Prep: 10 mins**   **Cook: 25–30 mins**

Ingredients

500 g/1 lb 2 oz
long-grain rice

2 tbsp groundnut oil

4 large eggs, lightly beaten

650 g/1 lb 7 oz fresh
beef mince

1 large onion,
finely chopped

2 garlic cloves,
finely chopped

140 g/5 oz frozen peas

3 tbsp light soy sauce

1 tsp sugar

salt

Method

1 Cook the rice in a large saucepan of salted boiling water for 15 minutes, until tender. Drain the rice, rinse with boiling water and set aside.

2 Heat a wok over a medium heat, then add the oil, swirl it around the wok and heat. Add the eggs and cook, stirring constantly, for 50–60 seconds, until set. Transfer to a dish and set aside.

3 Add the beef to the wok and stir-fry, breaking it up with a wooden spoon, for 4–5 minutes, until evenly browned. Stir in the onion, garlic and peas and stir-fry for a further 3–4 minutes.

4 Add the rice, soy sauce, sugar and eggs and cook, stirring constantly, for a further 1–2 minutes, until heated through. Serve immediately.

APPETIZERS & SIDE DISHES

PORK & CUCUMBER SALAD

Serves: 4   **Prep: 25 mins,**   **Cook: 6 mins**
                    plus marinating

Ingredients

450 g/1 lb pork tenderloin

6 spring onions, halved
lengthways and sliced
into 3

1 ridge cucumber

4 handfuls shredded
crisp lettuce

20 g/¾ oz
coriander leaves

10 g/¼ oz mint leaves

4 tbsp dry-roasted peanuts,
lightly crushed

finely grated zest of 1 lime

pinch of salt

1 tsp sugar

2 tsp sesame oil

1 tbsp groundnut oil

Marinade

2 small red chillies,
deseeded and very
finely chopped

4 tbsp sugar

3 tbsp Thai fish sauce

4 tbsp lime juice

4 tbsp rice vinegar

Method

1 Trim the tenderloin of any sinew and fat, and
thinly slice diagonally. Cut each slice in half
lengthways. Put in a bowl with the spring onions.
Peel the cucumber, halve lengthways and scoop
out the seeds. Thinly slice diagonally and put in
a bowl.

2 Next make the marinade. Using a large mortar
and pestle, pound the chopped chillies and the
sugar to a watery red paste. Add the fish sauce,
lime juice and rice vinegar, stirring to dissolve the
sugar. Pour into a measuring jug. Pour one half
over the pork and onions, and one half over the
cucumber. Leave to marinate for 1 hour, then
drain the cucumber reserving the marinade.

3 Put the shredded lettuce, coriander and mint
in a bowl, and toss to mix. Divide between
individual serving plates. Arrange the cucumber
slices on top and dress with the reserved
marinade.

4 Mix the nuts with the lime zest, salt and sugar.

5 Drain the pork and discard the marinade. Heat
a wok over a high heat, then add the oils. Stir-fry
the pork for 5 minutes until cooked through and
slightly caramelized. Arrange the pork slices on
top of the cucumber and sprinkle with the nut
mixture. Serve immediately.

STIR-FRIED BEANSPROUTS

Serves: 4   **Prep: 5 mins**   **Cook: 3 mins**

Ingredients

1 tbsp vegetable or
groundnut oil

225 g/8 oz fresh
beansprouts

2 tbsp spring onion,
finely chopped

½ tsp salt

pinch of sugar

Method

1 Heat a wok over a medium–high heat, then add the oil. Stir-fry the beansprouts with the spring onion for about 1 minute. Add the salt and sugar and stir.

2 Remove from the heat and serve immediately.

APPETIZERS & SIDE DISHES

STIR-FRIED LONG BEANS WITH RED PEPPER

Serves: 4-6   **Prep: 10 mins**   **Cook: 3-4 mins**

Ingredients

280 g/10 oz long beans, cut
into 6-cm/2½-inch lengths

1 tbsp vegetable or
groundnut oil

1 red pepper, slivered

pinch of salt

pinch of sugar

Method

1 Blanch the beans in a large pan of boiling water for 30 seconds. Drain and set aside.

2 In a preheated wok, heat the oil and stir-fry the beans for 1 minute over a high heat. Add the pepper and stir-fry for 1 more minute. Sprinkle the salt and sugar on top and serve immediately.

APPETIZERS & SIDE DISHES

CRAB WONTONS

Makes: 20

Prep: 20 mins,
plus cooling

Cook: 17 mins

Ingredients

1 tbsp groundnut or vegetable oil, plus extra for deep-frying

2.5-cm/1-inch piece fresh ginger, peeled and finely chopped

¼ red pepper, deseeded and finely chopped

handful of fresh coriander, chopped

¼ tsp salt

150 g/5½ oz canned white crabmeat, drained

20 wonton wrappers

water, for brushing

sweet chilli dipping sauce, to serve

Method

1 Heat 1 tablespoon of the oil in a preheated wok. Add the ginger and red pepper and stir-fry over a high heat for 30 seconds. Add the coriander and mix well. Leave to cool, then add the salt and the crabmeat and mix well.

2 Meanwhile remove the wrappers from the packet, but keep in a pile covered with clingfilm to prevent them from drying out. Lay one wrapper on a work surface in front of you and brush the edges with water. Put a teaspoonful of the crabmeat mixture in the centre and fold the wrapper over the mixture to form a triangle.

3 Press the edges together to seal. Fold each side corner up to the top corner to make a small parcel, brushing the edges with water to seal if necessary. Repeat with the remaining wrappers and crabmeat mixture.

4 Heat enough oil for deep-frying in a wok until it reaches 180–190°C/350–375°F, or until a cube of bread browns in 30 seconds. Add the wontons, in batches, and cook for 45–60 seconds until crisp and golden all over.

5 Remove with a slotted spoon, drain on kitchen paper and keep warm while you cook the remaining wontons. Serve with sweet chilli dipping sauce.

SWEET & SOUR SPARE RIBS

Serves: 4 **Prep: 15 mins,** plus marinating **Cook: 30 mins**

Ingredients

450 g/1 lb spare ribs, cut into bite-sized pieces

vegetable or groundnut oil, for deep-frying, plus 1½ tbsp, for stir-frying

1 green pepper, roughly chopped

1 small onion, roughly chopped

1 small carrot, finely sliced

½ tsp finely chopped garlic

½ tsp finely chopped fresh ginger

100 g/3½ oz pineapple chunks

Marinade

2 tsp light soy sauce

½ tsp salt

pinch of white pepper

Sauce

3 tbsp white rice vinegar

2 tbsp sugar

1 tbsp light soy sauce

1 tbsp tomato ketchup

Method

1 To make the marinade, combine the marinade ingredients in a bowl with the spare ribs and marinate for at least 20 minutes.

2 Heat enough oil for deep-frying in a wok until it reaches 180–190°C/350–375°F, or until a cube of bread browns in 30 seconds. Deep-fry the spare ribs for 8 minutes. Drain and set aside.

3 To prepare the sauce, mix together the vinegar, sugar, light soy sauce and ketchup. Set aside.

4 In a preheated wok, heat 1 tablespoon of the oil and stir-fry the pepper, onion and carrot for 2 minutes. Remove and set aside. Wipe the wok clean.

5 In the clean preheated wok, heat ½ tablespoon oil and stir-fry the garlic and ginger until fragrant. Add the sauce. Bring to the boil and add the pineapple chunks. Finally add the spare ribs and the pepper, onion and carrot. Stir until warmed through and serve immediately.

TWICE-FRIED SPARE RIBS

Serves: 4–6

Prep: 25 mins,   **Cook: 25 mins**
plus marinating & standing

Ingredients

1 kg/2 lb 4 oz spare ribs, chopped into 5-cm/ 2-inch pieces

groundnut oil, for deep-frying

juice of 1 lime

lime wedges and coriander leaves, to garnish

Marinade

3 tbsp clear honey

3 tbsp rice wine or dry sherry

1 tbsp soy sauce

1 tbsp rice vinegar or white wine vinegar

4 tbsp hoisin sauce

2.5-cm/1-inch piece fresh ginger, squeezed in a garlic press

½ tsp pepper

¼ tsp five spice

Seasoned flour

4 tbsp plain flour

½ tsp pepper

Method

1 To make the marinade, combine all the ingredients in a shallow dish. Add the ribs, turning to coat. Cover and leave to marinate in the refrigerator for at least 4 hours or up to 24 hours. Remove from the refrigerator and leave to come to room temperature before cooking.

2 Drain the ribs, discarding the marinade, and arrange in a single layer on a tray. Combine the seasoned flour ingredients in a shallow bowl.

3 Heat enough oil for deep-frying in a large wok until it reaches 180–190°C/350–375°F, or until a cube of bread browns in 30 seconds. When ready to fry, dredge the ribs with the seasoned flour, turning to coat. Fry in two batches for 3–4 minutes per batch, or until starting to brown round the edges. Drain thoroughly on kitchen paper.

4 Reheat the oil to 180°C/350°F. Add all the ribs to the wok and fry for a further 3–4 minutes, until crisp and slightly blackened round the edges and cooked through. Drain again on kitchen paper.

5 Tip the ribs into a warmed serving dish. Sprinkle with the lime juice, garnish with the lime wedges and coriander leaves and serve immediately.

HOT & SOUR COURGETTES

Serves: 4

Prep: 15–20 mins, **Cook: 5 mins**
plus standing & draining

Ingredients

2 large courgettes,
thinly sliced

1 tsp salt

2 tbsp groundnut oil

1 tsp Sichuan
peppercorns, crushed

½ –1 red chilli, deseeded
and sliced into thin strips

1 large garlic clove,
thinly sliced

½ tsp finely chopped
fresh ginger

1 tbsp rice vinegar

1 tbsp light soy sauce

2 tsp sugar

1 spring onion, green part
included, thinly sliced

a few drops of sesame oil,
to garnish

1 tsp sesame seeds,
to garnish

Method

1 Put the courgette slices in a large colander and toss with the salt. Cover with a plate and put a weight on top. Leave to drain for 20 minutes. Rinse off the salt and spread out the slices on kitchen paper to dry.

2 Preheat a wok over a high heat and add the oil. Add the Sichuan peppercorns, chilli, garlic and ginger. Fry for about 20 seconds until the garlic is just beginning to colour.

3 Add the courgette slices and toss in the oil. Add the rice vinegar, soy sauce and sugar, and stir-fry for 2 minutes. Add the spring onion and fry for 30 seconds. Garnish with the sesame oil and seeds, and serve immediately.

LAMB WITH SATAY SAUCE

Serves: 4

Prep: 20 mins,
plus marinating

Cook: 25 mins

Ingredients

450 g/1 lb lamb loin fillet

Marinade

1 tbsp mild curry paste

150 ml/5 fl oz coconut milk

2 garlic cloves, crushed

½ tsp chilli powder

½ tsp cumin

Satay sauce

1 tbsp corn oil

1 onion, diced

6 tbsp crunchy
peanut butter

1 tsp tomato purée

1 tsp fresh lime juice

100 ml/3½ fl oz cold water

Method

1 Using a sharp knife, thinly slice the lamb and place in a large dish.

2 To make the marinade, mix together the curry paste, coconut milk, garlic, chilli powder and cumin in a bowl. Pour over the lamb, toss well, cover and marinate for 30 minutes.

3 To make the satay sauce, heat the oil in a large preheated wok and stir-fry the onion for 5 minutes, then reduce the heat and cook for 5 minutes. Stir in the peanut butter, tomato purée, lime juice and water. Remove from the heat and set aside.

4 Thread the lamb on to pre-soaked wooden skewers, reserving the marinade. Preheat the grill to a medium–high heat and grill the lamb skewers under the grill for 6–8 minutes, turning once.

5 Add the reserved marinade to the wok, bring to the boil and cook for 5 minutes. Serve the lamb skewers with the marinade poured over the top and the satay sauce on the side.

APPETIZERS & SIDE DISHES

AUBERGINE WITH MISO

Serves: 4–6   **Prep: 10–15 mins**   **Cook: 16–18 mins**

Ingredients

2 tbsp groundnut oil

2 aubergines, cut into wedges

1 red chilli, sliced

2 tbsp sake

4 tbsp mirin

2 tbsp shoyu (Japanese soy sauce)

3 tbsp hatcho miso

2 tbsp water

Method

1 Preheat a wok over a high heat, add the oil and heat until very hot. Stir-fry the aubergine, in batches, for 4 minutes, or until browned and cooked through. Add more oil for each batch, if necessary.

2 Return all the aubergine to the wok together with the chilli and stir together. Add the remaining ingredients and toss everything together. Cook, stirring, until the sauce thickens. Serve immediately.

APPETIZERS & SIDE DISHES

STIR-FRIED BROCCOLI

Serves: 4   **Prep: 15 mins**   **Cook: 8–10 mins**

Ingredients

2 tbsp vegetable oil

2 medium heads of broccoli, cut into florets

1 tsp sesame seeds, toasted, to garnish

Sauce

2 tbsp soy sauce

1 tsp cornflour

1 tbsp caster sugar

1 tsp grated fresh ginger

1 garlic clove, crushed

pinch of hot chilli flakes

Method

1 In a large preheated wok, heat the oil until almost smoking. Stir-fry the broccoli for 4–5 minutes.

2 To make the sauce, combine the soy sauce, cornflour, sugar, ginger, garlic and hot chilli flakes in a small bowl. Add the sauce to the broccoli. Cook over a gentle heat, stirring constantly, for 2–3 minutes until the sauce thickens slightly.

3 Transfer to a warmed serving dish, garnish with the sesame seeds and serve immediately.

APPETIZERS & SIDE DISHES

SPICY FRENCH BEANS

Serves: 4　　　　**Prep: 10 mins**　　　　**Cook: 10 mins**

Ingredients

200 g/7 oz French beans

2 tbsp vegetable or groundnut oil

4 dried chillies, cut into 2–3 pieces

½ tsp Sichuan peppercorns

1 garlic clove, finely sliced

6 thin slices fresh ginger

2 spring onions, cut diagonally into thin pieces

pinch of sea salt

Method

1 Blanch the beans in a large pan of boiling water for 30 seconds. Drain and set aside.

2 Heat a wok over a medium–high heat, then add 1 tablespoon of the oil. Stir-fry the beans for about 5 minutes, or until they are beginning to wrinkle. Remove from the wok and set aside.

3 Add the remaining oil to the wok and stir-fry the chillies and Sichuan peppercorns until they are fragrant. Add the garlic, ginger and spring onions, and stir-fry until they begin to soften. Add the beans and toss to mix, then add the sea salt and serve immediately.

APPETIZERS & SIDE DISHES

CRISPY 'SEAWEED'

Serves: 4

Prep: 15 mins,
plus drying

Cook: 15–20 mins

Ingredients

250 g/9 oz dark green cabbage leaves

groundnut oil, for deep-frying

1 tsp caster sugar

½ tsp salt

4 tbsp flaked almonds, to garnish

Method

1 Remove and discard the tough stalks from the cabbage leaves. Wash the leaves, drain thoroughly and spread out on kitchen paper to dry. Stack a few leaves and roll up tightly. Using a very sharp knife, slice crossways into the thinnest possible shreds. Repeat with the remaining leaves. Spread out the shreds on kitchen paper and leave until completely dry.

2 Heat enough oil for deep-frying in a large wok until it reaches 180–190°C/350–375°F, or until a cube of bread browns in 30 seconds. Remove the wok from the heat and add half the shredded leaves. Return the wok to the heat and deep-fry until the shreds begin to float to the surface and become crisp. Remove with a slotted spoon and drain on kitchen paper. Keep warm while you deep-fry the rest.

3 Tip the shreds into a warm serving bowl. Combine the sugar and salt, and sprinkle over the 'seaweed', tossing to mix.

4 Quickly fry the flaked almonds in the hot oil. Remove with a slotted spoon and sprinkle over the 'seaweed'. Serve warm or at room temperature.

TEMPURA VEGETABLES

Serves: 4   **Prep: 20 mins**   **Cook: 25–35 mins**

Ingredients

150 g/5½ oz packet
tempura mix

4 shiitake mushrooms

4 fresh asparagus spears

4 slices sweet potato

1 red pepper, deseeded
and cut into strips

4 onion slices, cut widthwise
into rings

groundnut oil,
for deep-frying

Dipping sauce

2 tsp mirin

1 tbsp shoyu
(Japanese soy sauce)

pinch of dashi granules,
dissolved in 2 tbsp
boiling water

Method

1 To make the dipping sauce, mix together the ingredients in a small dipping dish.

2 Mix the tempura with water according to the packet instructions.

3 Drop the vegetables into the batter.

4 Heat enough oil for deep-frying in a wok until it reaches 180–190°C/350–375°F, or until a cube of bread browns in 30 seconds. Lift 2–3 pieces of the vegetables out of the batter, add to the oil, and cook for 2–3 minutes, or until the batter is a light golden colour.

5 Remove the tempura vegetables with a slotted spoon and drain on kitchen paper. Keep hot while you cook the remaining pieces.

6 Transfer the tempura vegetables to a serving dish and serve with the dipping sauce.

PORK BELLY ON CHINESE LEAVES

Serves: 4–6

Prep: 25–30 mins, plus marinating & cooling   **Cook: 1 hour 2 mins**

Ingredients

4 strips boneless pork belly, about 650 g/1 lb 7 oz in total

2 tbsp groundnut oil

6 tbsp chicken stock

1 thin slice fresh ginger

½ head Chinese leaves, sliced diagonally into ribbons

6 spring onions, green parts included, sliced diagonally into 4-cm/1½-inch pieces

½ tsp sugar

Marinade

2 tbsp sugar

2 tbsp Chinese rice wine or dry sherry

1 tbsp soy sauce

4-cm/1½-inch piece fresh ginger, roughly chopped and squeezed in a garlic press

¼ tsp five spice

4 tbsp hoisin sauce

Method

1 Using the tip of a very sharp knife, score the pork rind at 1-cm/½-inch intervals. Combine the marinade ingredients, pour the mixture into a dish and add the pork, rubbing the marinade into the slashes. Leave to stand at room temperature for 1 hour, turning occasionally.

2 Preheat the oven to 220°C/425°F/Gas Mark 7. Line a small roasting tin with foil and put a rack in it. Reserving the marinade, place the pork on the rack and put the tin on the top shelf of the oven. Roast for 15 minutes, then reduce the oven temperature to 180°C/350°F/Gas Mark 4. Turn the pork over and brush with the marinade. Roast for 20 minutes, then turn, brush with the marinade again and roast for a further 20 minutes until cooked through. Remove from the oven and leave to cool. Diagonally slice the pork into 1-cm/½-inch pieces. Put in a bowl and mix with the remaining marinade.

3 Heat a wok over a high heat, then add 1 tablespoon of the oil. Add the pork slices and marinade, and stir-fry for 2 minutes, until the marinade is reduced and bubbling. Pour in the stock, scraping up any sediment. Stir-fry for 2 minutes, until reduced. Remove from the wok and keep warm. Wipe out the wok with kitchen paper.

APPETIZERS & SIDE DISHES

4 Heat the wok over a high heat, then add the remaining oil. Add the ginger and stir-fry for a few seconds. Add the Chinese leaves, spring onions and sugar, and stir-fry for 1 minute, until just cooked and still brightly coloured.

5 Transfer the vegetables to a warmed serving dish. Pour the pork and juices over the top and serve immediately.

CHILLIES STUFFED WITH FISH PASTE

Serves: 4–6   **Prep: 20 mins,** plus marinating   **Cook: 17–20 mins**

Ingredients

225 g/8 oz white fish, minced

2 tbsp lightly beaten egg

4–6 mild large red and green chillies

vegetable or groundnut oil, for shallow-frying

2 garlic cloves, finely chopped

½ –1 tsp fermented black beans, rinsed and lightly mashed

1 tbsp light soy sauce

pinch of sugar

1 tbsp water

Marinade

1 tsp finely chopped fresh ginger

pinch of salt

pinch of white pepper

½ tsp vegetable or groundnut oil

Method

1 To make the marinade, combine all the ingredients in a bowl and marinate the fish for 20 minutes. Add the egg and mix by hand to create a smooth paste.

2 To prepare the chillies, cut in half lengthways and scoop out the seeds and loose flesh. Cut into bite-sized pieces. Spread each piece of chilli with about ½ teaspoon of the fish paste.

3 In a preheated wok, heat plenty of oil and cook the chilli pieces on both sides until beginning to turn golden brown. Drain the chillies, set aside and wipe the wok clean.

4 Heat 1 tablespoon of fresh oil in the clean wok and stir-fry the garlic until aromatic. Stir in the black beans and mix well. Add the light soy sauce and sugar and stir, then add the chilli pieces. Add the water, then cover and simmer over low heat for 5 minutes. Serve immediately.

ASIAN-STYLE GLAZED CHICKEN WINGS

Serves: 4–6

Prep: 20 mins, plus marinating

Cook: 15 mins

Ingredients

8 chicken wings, each wing chopped into 3 pieces

5 tbsp groundnut oil

6 tbsp chicken stock

2 tbsp chopped fresh coriander, to garnish

Marinade

1½ tbsp Chinese rice wine or dry sherry

1 tbsp soy sauce

1 tbsp rice vinegar

1½ tbsp sugar

⅛ tsp five spice

3 tbsp hoisin sauce

1 tsp finely chopped fresh ginger

Method

1 To make the marinade, combine the wine, soy sauce and vinegar in a small bowl. Add the sugar and five spice, and stir until dissolved. Mix in the hoisin sauce and ginger.

2 Put the chopped chicken wings in a shallow dish and pour in the marinade, turning the wings to coat. Leave to marinate for 1 hour at room temperature, or overnight in the refrigerator.

3 Heat a wok over a high heat, add the oil and when it is almost smoking add the chicken wings and marinade. Stir-fry for 5 minutes, then sprinkle with 4 tablespoons of the stock and stir-fry for a further 4 minutes, until the chicken is tender and the juices run clear when a skewer is inserted into the thickest part of the meat.

4 Using tongs, transfer the wings to a warmed serving dish and garnish with coriander. Pour off and discard most of the oil from the wok and return to the heat. Add the remaining 2 tablespoons of stock and stir with a wooden spoon until blended, scraping up the sticky sediment. Pour into a small bowl and serve with the wings as a dipping sauce.

HOT & SOUR VEGETABLE SALAD

Serves: 4   **Prep: 15–20 mins**   **Cook: 4–6 mins**

Ingredients

2 tbsp vegetable oil or groundnut oil

1 tbsp chilli oil

1 onion, sliced

2.5-cm/1-inch piece fresh ginger, grated

1 small head broccoli, cut into florets

2 carrots, cut into short thin sticks

1 red pepper, deseeded and cut into squares

1 yellow pepper, deseeded and cut into strips

55 g/2 oz mangetout, trimmed and halved

55 g/2 oz baby corn, halved

Dressing

2 tbsp vegetable oil or groundnut oil

1 tsp chilli oil

1 tbsp rice wine vinegar

juice of 1 lime

½ tsp Thai fish sauce

Method

1 Heat a wok over a medium–high heat and add the oils. Add the onion and ginger and sauté for 1–2 minutes until they start to soften. Add the remaining vegetables and stir-fry for 2–3 minutes until they have softened slightly. Remove from the heat and set aside.

2 Mix together the dressing ingredients. Transfer the vegetables to a serving plate and drizzle the dressing over. Serve warm, or allow the flavours to develop and serve cold.

APPETIZERS & SIDE DISHES

PORK MEATBALLS IN LEMON GRASS & CHILLI BROTH WITH PAK CHOI

Serves: 4

Prep: 25–30 mins, plus cooling & chilling

Cook: 25–30 mins

Ingredients

1.2 litres/2 pints chicken stock

¼ –½ fresh red chilli, deseeded and very finely sliced

½ tsp palm sugar

3 fresh thyme sprigs

2 lemon grass stalks, fibrous outer leaves removed, stems bashed with the flat of a knife

¼ tsp pepper

6 tbsp groundnut oil

1 small head pak choi, stems cut into small squares, leaves sliced into ribbons

1 spring onion, green parts included, sliced diagonally

soy sauce

salt and pepper

lime wedges, to garnish

Pork meatballs

225 g/8 oz fresh pork mince

1 shallot, grated

2-cm/¾-inch piece fresh ginger, squeezed in a garlic press

1 garlic clove, crushed

finely grated zest and juice of ½ lime

Method

1 Pour the stock into a medium-sized wok or saucepan. Add the chilli, sugar, thyme, lemon grass and pepper. Season to taste with salt and bring to the boil. Reduce the heat and simmer gently for 10 minutes. Remove from the heat and leave to cool for about 30 minutes.

2 To make the pork meatballs, combine the pork, shallot, ginger, garlic, lime zest and juice and season with salt and pepper. Mix well with a fork.

3 Line a plate with kitchen paper. Divide the mixture into 16–20 walnut-sized balls. Place on the prepared plate and chill for 30 minutes.

4 Heat a large wok over a high heat. Add the oil and heat until very hot. Add the pork meatballs and fry for 5–6 minutes, until golden brown all over and cooked through. Drain on kitchen paper and keep warm.

5 Remove the thyme and lemon grass from the broth. Add the pak choi and spring onion. Bring to the boil then simmer for 2 minutes until the pak choi stalks are just tender. Season with a splash of soy sauce.

6 Divide the pork meatballs between warmed soup bowls. Ladle the broth and vegetables over, garnish with lime wedges and serve immediately.

APPETIZERS & SIDE DISHES

WOK-FRIED KING PRAWNS IN SPICY SAUCE

Serves: 4　　　　**Prep: 10 mins**　　　　**Cook: 10 mins**

Ingredients

3 tbsp vegetable or groundnut oil

450 g/1 lb raw king prawns, unpeeled

2 tsp finely chopped fresh ginger

1 tsp finely chopped garlic

1 tbsp chopped spring onion

2 tbsp chilli bean sauce

1 tsp Shaoxing rice wine

1 tsp sugar

½ tsp light soy sauce

½ tbsp chicken stock

Method

1　Heat a wok over a high heat, then add the oil. Add the prawns and stir-fry for 4 minutes, until they turn pink and start to curl. Arrange the prawns on the sides of the wok out of the oil, then add the ginger and garlic and stir until fragrant. Add the spring onion and chilli bean sauce and stir the prawns back into the mixture.

2　Reduce the heat slightly and add the rice wine, sugar, light soy sauce and chicken stock. Cover and cook for a further minute until the prawns are cooked through. Serve immediately.

APPETIZERS & SIDE DISHES

MINCED PORK KEBABS WITH SWEET CHILLI DIPPING SAUCE

Makes: 8

Prep: 20 mins,
plus chilling

Cook: 6–8 mins

Ingredients

1 large onion, chopped

2 garlic cloves, crushed

450 g/1 lb minced pork

1 tsp salt

2 tbsp sweet chilli dipping sauce, plus extra to serve

handful of fresh coriander, chopped, plus extra sprigs to garnish (optional)

1 egg

egg-fried rice, to serve

Method

1 Put all the ingredients except the rice in a food processor and process to a thick paste.

2 Divide the pork mixture into eight portions. Using damp hands, squeeze one portion evenly around a flat metal skewer, repeat to make eight kebabs. Cover and chill in the refrigerator for at least 1 hour.

3 Heat a ridged griddle pan over a medium–high heat, add the kebabs and cook, turning occasionally, for 5–6 minutes until browned all over and cooked through. Serve immediately on a bed of freshly cooked egg-tried rice with sweet chilli dipping sauce and garnished with sprigs of fresh coriander, if using.

APPETIZERS & SIDE DISHES

PORK & VEGETABLE BROTH

Serves: 4   **Prep: 15 mins**   **Cook: 45 mins**

Ingredients

1 tbsp chilli oil

1 garlic clove, chopped

3 spring onions, sliced

1 red pepper, deseeded and finely sliced

2 tbsp cornflour

1 litre/1¾ pints vegetable stock

1 tbsp soy sauce

2 tbsp rice wine or dry sherry

150 g/5½ oz pork fillet, sliced

1 tbsp finely chopped lemon grass

1 small red chilli, deseeded and finely chopped

1 tbsp grated fresh ginger

115 g/4 oz fine egg noodles

200 g/7 oz canned water chestnuts, drained and sliced

salt and pepper

Method

1 Heat a large wok over a high heat, then add the oil. Add the garlic and spring onions and stir-fry for 3 minutes until slightly soft. Add the red pepper and stir-fry for a further 5 minutes.

2 In a bowl, mix the cornflour with enough of the stock to make a smooth paste, then stir it into the pan. Cook, stirring, for 2 minutes. Stir in the remaining stock, the soy sauce and the rice wine, then add the pork, lemon grass, chilli and ginger. Season with salt and pepper. Bring to the boil, then reduce the heat and simmer for 25 minutes until the pork is cooked through.

3 Cook the noodles in a saucepan of boiling water for 3–4 minutes, or cook according to the packet instructions, until tender. Remove from the heat, drain, then add the noodles to the soup along with the water chestnuts. Cook for a further 2 minutes, then remove from the heat and ladle into warmed bowls.

JAPANESE-STYLE BEEF SOUP

Serves: 4   **Prep: 15–20 mins**   **Cook: 13–15 mins**

Ingredients

115 g/4 oz dried udon or soba noodles

2 tbsp brown rice miso

600 ml/1 pint vegetable stock

1 tbsp mirin or rice wine

85 g/3 oz baby corn, halved diagonally

85 g/3 oz button mushrooms, halved

85 g/3 oz beansprouts

40 g/1½ oz baby spinach leaves

1 tbsp groundnut or sunflower oil

280 g/10 oz thin-cut sirloin or rump steak, cut into bite-sized pieces

1 small red chilli, very thinly sliced

Method

1 Cook the noodles in a saucepan of boiling water for 3–4 minutes, or cook according to the packet instructions, until tender. Drain and set aside.

2 Blend the miso with a little of the stock. Heat the remaining stock in a saucepan. Add the mirin, baby corn and mushrooms, and simmer for 3 minutes. Add the beansprouts and simmer for a further 1 minute. Remove from the heat and stir in the miso. Add the spinach and cover the pan.

3 Heat a wok until very hot. Add the oil and stir-fry the steak with the chilli for 1–2 minutes until browned, or cooked to your taste. Remove from the heat.

4 Pour boiling water over the noodles to reheat them. Drain well then divide between warmed bowls. Ladle the miso-flavoured soup and vegetables over the noodles. Top with the stir-fried beef and serve immediately.

HOT & SOUR SOUP TOM YUM

Serves: 4

Prep: 15 mins,
plus standing

Cook: 40–50 mins

Ingredients

2 fresh red chillies,
deseeded and roughly
chopped

6 tbsp rice vinegar

1.2 litres/2 pints
vegetable stock

2 lemon grass stalks, halved

4 tbsp soy sauce

1 tbsp palm sugar

juice of ½ lime

2 tbsp groundnut or
vegetable oil

225 g/8 oz firm tofu
(drained weight), cut into
1-cm/½-inch cubes

400 g/14 oz canned straw
mushrooms, drained

4 spring onions, chopped

1 small head pak
choi, shredded

Method

1 Mix together the chillies and vinegar in a
non-reactive bowl, cover and leave to stand at
room temperature for 1 hour.

2 Meanwhile, bring the stock to the boil in a
saucepan. Add the lemon grass, soy sauce, sugar
and lime juice, reduce the heat and simmer for
20–30 minutes.

3 Heat the oil in a preheated wok, add the
tofu cubes and stir-fry over a high heat for
2–3 minutes, or until browned all over. (You may
need to do this in 2 batches, depending on the
size of the wok.) Remove with a slotted spoon
and drain on kitchen paper.

4 Add the chilli and vinegar mixture with the tofu,
mushrooms and half the spring onions to the
broth and cook for 10 minutes.

5 Mix the remaining spring onions with the
pak choi.

6 Scatter over the spring onions and pak choi
and serve immediately.

APPETIZERS & SIDE DISHES

CHICKEN NOODLE SOUP

Serves: 4　　　**Prep: 15 mins**　　　**Cook: 25–30 mins**

Ingredients

1 tbsp corn oil

4 skinless, boneless chicken thighs, diced

1 bunch of spring onions, sliced, white and green kept separate

2 garlic cloves, chopped

2-cm/¾-inch piece fresh ginger, finely chopped

850 ml/1½ pints chicken stock

175 ml/6 fl oz coconut milk

3 tsp Thai red curry paste

3 tbsp peanut butter

2 tbsp light soy sauce

1 small red pepper, deseeded and chopped

55 g/2 oz frozen peas

250 g/9 oz medium egg noodles

salt and pepper

Method

1 Heat a wok over a medium–high heat, then add the oil. Add the chicken and stir-fry for 5 minutes, or until lightly browned. Add the white part of the spring onions, the garlic and ginger, and stir-fry for 2 minutes.

2 Add the stock, coconut milk, curry paste, peanut butter and soy sauce. Season to taste with salt and pepper. Bring to the boil, stirring constantly, then simmer for 8 minutes, stirring occasionally, until the chicken is cooked through. Add the pepper, peas and green spring onion tops and cook for a further 2 minutes.

3 Cook the noodles in a saucepan of boiling water for 3–4 minutes, or cook according to the packet instructions, until tender. Drain the noodles, then add them to the wok and heat through. Spoon into soup bowls and serve immediately.

★ **Variation**

Rice noodles would be a good alternative to wheat-based egg noodles for anyone following a gluten-free diet.

HOISIN PORK WITH GARLIC NOODLES

Serves: 4 **Prep: 15–20 mins** **Cook: 15 mins**

Ingredients

250 g/9 oz dried thick Chinese egg noodles, or Chinese wholemeal egg noodles

450 g/1 lb pork fillet, thinly sliced

1 tsp sugar

1 tbsp groundnut or corn oil

4 tbsp rice vinegar

4 tbsp white wine vinegar

4 tbsp hoisin sauce

2 spring onions, sliced on the diagonal

about 2 tbsp garlic-flavoured corn oil

2 large garlic cloves, thinly sliced

chopped fresh coriander, to garnish

Method

1 Boil the noodles for 3–4 minutes, or cook according to the packet instructions, until soft. Rinse under cold water, drain well and set aside.

2 Meanwhile, sprinkle the pork slices with the sugar and toss together. Heat the oil in a preheated wok, add the pork and stir-fry for about 3 minutes until the pork is cooked through and is no longer pink. Remove with a slotted spoon and keep warm. Add the vinegars to the wok and boil until they are reduced to about 5 tablespoons. Pour in the hoisin sauce, add the spring onions and let it bubble until reduced by half. Add to the pork and stir together.

3 Quickly wipe out the wok, heat the garlic-flavoured oil, then add the garlic slices and stir-fry for about 30 seconds, until they are golden and crisp. Remove with a slotted spoon and set aside.

4 Add the noodles to the wok and stir to warm them through. Divide between four plates, top with the pork and spring onion mixture, then sprinkle over the garlic slices and coriander.

★ Variation

Stir 1 tablespoon of peanut butter into the pan with the hoisin sauce for added flavour. Garnish with cashew nut halves or peanuts.

MEAT

SWEET & SOUR PORK

Serves: 4   **Prep: 15–20 mins**   **Cook: 25–30 mins**

Ingredients

150 ml/5 fl oz vegetable oil, for deep-frying

225 g/8 oz pork fillet, cut into 1-cm/½-inch cubes

1 onion, sliced

1 green pepper, deseeded and sliced

225 g/8 oz pineapple pieces

1 small carrot, cut into thin strips

25 g/1 oz canned bamboo shoots, drained, rinsed and halved

cooked rice, to serve

Batter

125 g/4½ oz plain flour

1 tbsp cornflour

1½ tsp baking powder

1 tbsp vegetable oil

Sauce

125 g/4½ oz soft light brown sugar

2 tbsp cornflour

125 ml/4 fl oz white wine vinegar

2 garlic cloves, crushed

4 tbsp tomato purée

6 tbsp pineapple juice

Method

1 To make the batter, sift the plain flour into a mixing bowl, together with the cornflour and baking powder. Add the oil and whisk in enough water (about 175 ml/6 fl oz) to make a thick, smooth batter. Heat enough oil for deep-frying in a large wok until it reaches 180–190°C/350–375°F, or until a cube of bread browns in 30 seconds.

2 Dip the cubes of pork into the batter and cook in the hot oil, in batches, until the pork is cooked through. Remove the pork from the wok with a slotted spoon and drain on kitchen paper. Set aside and keep warm until required.

3 Drain all but 1 tablespoon of oil from the wok and return it to the heat. Add the onion, pepper, pineapple pieces, carrot and bamboo shoots and stir-fry for 1–2 minutes. Remove from the wok with a slotted spoon and set aside. Mix all of the sauce ingredients together and pour into the wok.

4 Bring to the boil, stirring until thickened and clear. Cook for 1 minute, then return the pork and vegetables to the wok. Cook for a further 1–2 minutes, then transfer to a serving plate and serve with freshly cooked rice.

MEAT

BEEF & PAK CHOI STIR-FRY

Serves: 4   **Prep: 15 mins,**   **Cook: 8 mins**
plus marinating

Ingredients

350 g/12 oz skirt steak

2 tbsp groundnut oil

1 shallot, chopped

2 tsp finely chopped
fresh ginger

1 fresh red chilli, deseeded
and thinly sliced

350 g/12 oz pak choi, stalks
cut into 2.5-cm/1-inch
squares and leaves sliced
into wide ribbons

1 tbsp cornflour

2 tbsp beef stock or water

Marinade

2 tbsp soy sauce

1½ tbsp Chinese rice wine
or dry sherry

½ tsp sugar

½ tsp pepper

Method

1 Pound the steak with the blunt side of a knife.
Slice the steak into thin strips and put in a shallow
dish. Combine the marinade ingredients and
pour over the beef. Leave to marinate for
1 hour at room temperature, or overnight in the
refrigerator.

2 Heat a wok over a medium–high heat, then
add the oil. Stir-fry the shallot, ginger and chilli for
1 minute. Increase the heat to high and add the
beef and marinade. Stir-fry for 3 minutes. Add the
pak choi stalks and stir-fry for 1 minute. Add the
leaves and stir-fry for a further minute.

3 Mix the cornflour and stock to a smooth paste.
Add to the wok and stir-fry for 1 minute, until
slightly thickened. Transfer to a warmed serving
dish and serve immediately.

LAMB WITH LIME LEAVES

Serves: 4   **Prep: 15 mins**   **Cook: 35 mins**

Ingredients

450 g/1 lb lean boneless lamb (leg or loin fillet)

2 tbsp groundnut or vegetable oil

2 fresh bird's eye chillies, deseeded and finely chopped

2 garlic cloves, crushed

4 shallots, chopped

2 lemon grass stalks, sliced

6 fresh kafir lime leaves

1 tbsp tamarind paste

2 tbsp palm sugar or soft light brown sugar

300 ml/10 fl oz canned coconut milk

175 g/6 oz cherry tomatoes, halved

1 tbsp chopped fresh coriander, plus extra to garnish

cooked rice, to serve

Method

1 Using a sharp knife, cut the lamb into thin strips or cubes. Heat a wok over a high heat, then add the oil. Add the chillies, garlic, shallots, lemon grass, lime leaves, tamarind paste and sugar.

2 Add the lamb to the wok and stir-fry for 5 minutes, tossing well so that the lamb is evenly coated in the spice mixture.

3 Pour the coconut milk into the wok and bring to the boil. Reduce the heat and simmer for 20 minutes.

4 Add the cherry tomatoes and coriander to the wok and simmer for 5 minutes.

5 Transfer to individual serving plates, sprinkle with coriander and serve immediately with freshly cooked rice.

MEAT

SICHUAN PORK, AUBERGINE & CHILLI STIR-FRY

Serves: 4 **Prep: 20 mins** **Cook: 30–35 mins**

Ingredients

2 aubergines, about 350 g/12 oz each

2 tbsp groundnut oil, plus extra for brushing

3–4 tbsp Sichuan chilli bean paste

2.5-cm/1-inch piece fresh ginger, very finely chopped

2 large garlic cloves, very finely chopped

500 g/1 lb 2 oz fresh pork mince

1 tsp sugar

2 tbsp soy sauce

1 tbsp Chinese black vinegar or thin balsamic vinegar

2 tsp Sichuan peppercorns

10 spring onions, green parts included, chopped

¾ tsp cornflour

125 ml/4 fl oz chicken stock

1 tbsp sesame seeds

salt

shredded spring onion, green parts included, to garnish

Method

1 Halve the aubergines lengthways, then slice diagonally into 15-mm/⅝-inch slices. Halve the larger slices. Lightly brush or spray the aubergine slices with oil.

2 Heat a wok over a medium–high heat, then lightly brush or spray with oil and heat until almost smoking. Add the aubergine slices in batches and stir-fry, tossing, for 30 seconds. Reduce the heat to medium, and continue to stir-fry, tossing, for a further 5–7 minutes, until brown, taking care they do not burn. Remove each slice from the wok once brown, set aside and keep warm while cooking the remaining slices.

3 Wipe out the wok with kitchen paper. Add the oil and heat until very hot, then add the chilli bean paste. Stir vigorously over a medium–high heat for 30 seconds to amalgamate the oil with the paste.

4 Add the ginger and garlic and stir-fry for 30 seconds. Add the pork, using a wooden spoon to break up the meat. Stir-fry for 2 minutes, until the pork is cooked through and no longer pink.

5 Stir in the sugar, soy sauce, vinegar, peppercorns, and salt to taste. Add the aubergines and spring onions and stir-fry for 3 minutes.

MEAT

6 Mix the cornflour to a smooth paste with a little of the stock. Add to the wok, stir briefly, then add the remaining stock. Cook for 1 minute, until the sauce has thickened.

7 Transfer to warmed serving bowls, sprinkle with the sesame seeds, garnish with shredded spring onion and serve immediately.

HOT SESAME BEEF

Serves: 4 **Prep: 15–20 mins** **Cook: 10–15 mins**

Ingredients

500 g/1 lb 2 oz fillet steak, cut into thin strips

1½ tbsp sesame seeds

125 ml/4 fl oz beef stock

2 tbsp soy sauce

2 tbsp grated fresh ginger

2 garlic cloves, finely chopped

1 tsp cornflour

½ tsp chilli flakes

3 tbsp sesame oil

1 large head of broccoli, cut into florets

1 yellow pepper, deseeded and thinly sliced

1 fresh red chilli, finely sliced

1 tbsp chilli oil, or to taste

coriander, to garnish

cooked wild rice, to serve

Method

1 Mix the beef strips with 1 tablespoon of the sesame seeds in a small bowl.

2 In a separate bowl, stir together the stock, soy sauce, ginger, garlic, cornflour and chilli flakes.

3 Heat 1 tablespoon of the sesame oil in a large wok. Stir-fry the beef strips for 2–3 minutes. Remove and set aside, then wipe the wok with kitchen paper.

4 Heat the remaining sesame oil in the wok, add the broccoli, yellow pepper, red chilli and chilli oil and stir-fry for 2–3 minutes.

5 Stir in the stock mixture, cover and simmer for 2 minutes.

6 Return the beef to the wok and simmer until the juices thicken, stirring occasionally. Cook for a further 1–2 minutes. Sprinkle with the remaining sesame seeds.

7 Garnish with chopped fresh coriander and serve over freshly cooked wild rice.

MEAT

SPICY SICHUAN PORK

Serves: 4

Prep: 10-15 mins, plus cooling

Cook: 30-35 mins

Ingredients

280 g/10 oz pork belly, thinly sliced

1 tbsp vegetable or groundnut oil

1 tbsp chilli bean sauce

1 tbsp fermented black beans, rinsed and lightly mashed

1 tsp sweet red bean paste (optional)

1 green pepper, deseeded and finely sliced

1 red pepper, deseeded and finely sliced

1 tsp sugar

1 tsp dark soy sauce

pinch of white pepper

Method

1 Bring a saucepan of water to the boil and place the pork slices in the pan, then cover and simmer for about 20 minutes, skimming occasionally. Leave the pork to cool.

2 Heat a wok over a medium–high heat, then add the oil. Stir-fry the pork slices until they begin to shrink. Stir in the chilli bean sauce, then add the black beans and the red bean paste, if using.

3 Add the peppers and the remaining ingredients and stir-fry for a couple of minutes, or until the peppers have softened and the pork is cooked through. Serve immediately.

MEAT

MARINATED BEEF WITH VEGETABLES

Serves: 4

Prep: 15 mins, plus marinating

Cook: 8 mins

Ingredients

500 g/1 lb 2 oz rump steak

3 tbsp sesame oil

½ tbsp cornflour

½ tbsp soy sauce

1 head of broccoli, cut into florets

2 carrots, cut into thin strips

125 g/4½ oz mangetout

125 ml/4 fl oz beef stock

250 g/9 oz baby spinach, shredded

Marinade

1 tbsp dry sherry

½ tbsp soy sauce

½ tbsp cornflour

½ tsp caster sugar

2 garlic cloves, finely chopped

1 tbsp sesame oil

Method

1 Trim any fat from the steak. Slice the meat into thin strips and put in a shallow dish. Combine the marinade ingredients and pour over the beef. Leave to marinate for 30 minutes, then remove the beef and discard the marinade.

2 Heat a wok over a medium–high heat, then add 1 tablespoon of the oil. Stir-fry the beef for 2 minutes. Remove from the wok and set aside.

3 Combine the cornflour and soy sauce in a bowl and set aside. Pour the remaining 2 tablespoons of oil into the wok, add the broccoli, carrots and mangetout and stir-fry for 2 minutes.

4 Add the stock, cover the wok and cook for 1 minute. Stir in the spinach, beef and the cornflour mixture. Cook until the juices boil and thicken. Serve immediately.

MEAT

SLICED BEEF IN BLACK BEAN SAUCE

Serves: 4   **Prep: 10–15 mins**   **Cook: 6–8 mins**

Ingredients

3 tbsp groundnut oil

450 g/1 lb beef sirloin, thinly sliced

1 red pepper, deseeded and thinly sliced

1 green pepper, deseeded and thinly sliced

1 bunch spring onions, sliced

2 garlic cloves, crushed

1 tbsp grated fresh ginger

2 tbsp black bean sauce

1 tbsp sherry

1 tbsp soy sauce

Method

1 Heat a wok over a high heat, then add 2 tablespoons of the oil. Add the beef and stir-fry for 1–2 minutes, then remove and set aside.

2 Add the remaining oil and peppers and stir-fry for 2 minutes. Add the spring onions, garlic and ginger and stir-fry for 30 seconds.

3 Add the black bean sauce, sherry and soy sauce, then stir in the beef and heat until bubbling. Transfer to bowls and serve.

MEAT

PORK STIR-FRY WITH CASHEWS, LIME & MINT

Serves: 2

Prep: 15–20 mins, plus standing

Cook: 8–10 mins

Ingredients

280 g/10 oz pork fillet

1 tsp coriander seeds

½ tsp white peppercorns

¼ tsp salt

¼ tsp sugar

juice and finely grated rind of 1 lime

2 tbsp groundnut oil

1 tsp finely chopped fresh ginger

1 garlic clove, thinly sliced

3 spring onions, white and green parts separated, then halved lengthways and sliced into 2-cm/¾-inch pieces

1 small green pepper, deseeded and thinly sliced

2 tbsp cashew nuts, roughly chopped

1 tbsp chicken stock

1 tsp Thai fish sauce

2 tbsp fresh mint, to garnish

Method

1 Diagonally slice the pork across the grain into thin bite-sized pieces. Flatten with the back of a knife or with a meat mallet. Using a mortar and pestle, crush the coriander seeds, peppercorns, salt, sugar and lime rind together. Spread the mixture over both sides of the pork, pressing it in well. Leave to stand for 15 minutes.

2 Heat a wok over a high heat, then add 1 tablespoon of the oil. Stir-fry the pork for 2–3 minutes until cooked through. Transfer to a plate with the juices. Wipe out the wok with kitchen paper.

3 Heat the wok over a medium–high heat, then add the remaining oil. Stir-fry the ginger and garlic for a few seconds. Add the white spring onion and green pepper, and stir-fry for 2 minutes. Add the cashew nuts, then stir-fry for a further minute.

4 Increase the heat to high, then return the pork and juices to the wok. Add the stock, lime juice, fish sauce and the green spring onion. Stir-fry for 30 seconds to heat through, then sprinkle with the mint and serve.

LAMB & LEEK STIR-FRY

Serves: 2

Prep: 15 mins,
plus marinating

Cook: 7 mins

Ingredients

280 g/10 oz lamb neck fillet

½ tbsp cornflour

2 tbsp chicken stock

2 tbsp groundnut oil

3 leeks, green part included, sliced into 4-cm/ 1½-inch pieces

pepper

Marinade

1 garlic clove, finely chopped

2 tsp soy sauce

2 tsp Chinese rice wine or dry sherry

½ tsp sugar

¼ tsp salt

Method

1 Diagonally slice the lamb across the grain into thin bite-sized pieces. Flatten with the back of a knife blade and put in a bowl. Combine the marinade ingredients and pour over the lamb. Leave to stand for 1 hour at room temperature, or overnight in the refrigerator.

2 Mix the cornflour and 1 tablespoon of the stock to a thin paste. Heat a wok over a high heat, then add 1 tablespoon of the oil. Add the lamb and stir-fry for 1 minute, then season to taste with pepper. Add the cornflour paste and stir-fry for a further minute. Remove from the wok and keep warm. Wipe out the wok with kitchen paper.

3 Heat the wok over a high heat, then add the remaining oil. Add the leeks and the remaining chicken stock, and stir-fry for 2 minutes, until just cooked and still bright green and crisp. Return the lamb to the wok and stir-fry for 30 seconds. Transfer to a warmed serving dish and serve immediately.

MEAT

BEEF WITH BLACK PEPPER & LIME

Serves: 2

Prep: 20 mins, plus marinating

Cook: 5 mins

Ingredients

350 g/12 oz skirt steak

½ tbsp palm sugar or light brown sugar

1 tbsp black peppercorns, crushed

4 tsp soy sauce

1 fresh red bird's eye chilli, deseeded and finely chopped

½ garlic bulb, divided into cloves and crushed

2 tbsp lime juice

½ head Chinese leaves, sliced

½ red onion, thinly sliced

1½ tbsp groundnut oil

½ tsp Thai fish sauce

handful fresh mint leaves

lime wedges, to garnish

Method

1 Pound the steak with the blunt side of a knife. Slice diagonally across the grain into thin, bite-sized pieces and place in a shallow bowl.

2 Combine the sugar, peppercorns, soy sauce, chilli, garlic and 1 tablespoon of the lime juice in a bowl, mixing well. Pour over the beef, stirring to coat. Leave to marinate for 1 hour at room temperature, or overnight in the refrigerator.

3 Arrange the Chinese leaves in a shallow serving dish. Scatter with the onion slices.

4 Heat a wok over a high heat, then add the oil. Add the meat and stir-fry for 3 minutes, then add the fish sauce and the remaining lime juice and stir-fry for a further minute.

5 Tip the beef and juices over the Chinese leaves and onion, then scatter over the mint. Garnish with lime wedges and serve immediately.

MEAT

BEEF, SPRING ONION & PAK CHOI STIR-FRY

Serves: 4 **Prep: 10-15 mins** **Cook: 9-12 mins**

Ingredients

1 tbsp groundnut oil

2 garlic cloves, crushed

2.5-cm/1-inch piece fresh ginger, chopped

400 g/14 oz lean steak mince

1 bunch spring onions, diagonally sliced

280 g/10 oz pak choi, thickly sliced

200 g/7 oz beansprouts

2 tbsp lime juice

2 tbsp tomato ketchup

2 tbsp soy sauce

cooked egg noodles, to serve

Method

1 Heat the oil in a wok, add the garlic and ginger, and stir-fry over a medium heat for a few seconds, without browning.

2 Increase the heat to high, stir in the mince and stir-fry for 4-5 minutes. Add the spring onions and pak choi and stir-fry for 2 minutes.

3 Add the beansprouts and stir-fry for 1-2 minutes until soft.

4 Stir in the lime juice, ketchup and soy sauce, then heat until bubbling. Serve with freshly cooked egg noodles.

MEAT

GREEN LAMB STIR-FRY WITH NOODLES AND PEANUTS

Serves: 4

Prep: 15–20 mins, plus marinating

Cook: 10–12 mins

Ingredients

450 g/1 lb boneless lamb

2 tbsp soy sauce

2 tsp cornflour

125 g/4½ oz dried egg noodles

3 tbsp groundnut oil

200 ml/7 fl oz chicken stock

1 tbsp Thai fish sauce

100 g/3½ oz Chinese garlic chives, or green stalks from 2 bunches of spring onions

2-cm/¾-inch piece galangal or fresh ginger, finely chopped

5 tbsp green curry paste

50 g/1¾ oz dry-roasted peanuts, roughly chopped

1 lime

salt

Method

1 Slice the lamb into 4 x 1-cm/1½ x ½-inch strips and put in a shallow dish. Sprinkle with the soy sauce, cornflour and a pinch of salt, tossing well to coat. Cover and leave to marinate in the refrigerator for 1–24 hours.

2 Cook the noodles according to the packet instructions. Drain, return to the pan, and toss with 1 tablespoon of the oil.

3 Meanwhile, combine the stock, fish sauce and ½ teaspoon of salt. Trim the garlic chives and slice into 2-cm/¾-inch lengths.

4 Heat a wok over a high heat. Add the remaining oil and stir-fry the lamb for 3 minutes or until no longer pink. Add the galangal and curry paste and stir-fry for 1 minute. Pour in the stock mixture and stir until boiling. Add the noodles, tossing to coat with the sauce. Add the chives and stir-fry for a few seconds until wilted. Sprinkle with the peanuts and juice from half the lime. Serve immediately with slices from the remaining lime.

MEAT

GINGER BEEF WITH YELLOW PEPPERS

Serves: 4

Prep: 15 mins,
plus marinating

Cook: 10 mins

Ingredients

500 g/1 lb 2 oz beef fillet

2 tsp groundnut oil

2 garlic cloves, crushed

2 tbsp grated fresh ginger

pinch of chilli flakes

2 yellow peppers,
deseeded and thinly sliced

125 g/4½ oz baby corn

175 g/6 oz mangetout

Marinade

2 tbsp soy sauce

2 tsp groundnut oil

1½ tsp caster sugar

1 tsp cornflour

Method

1 Slice the meat into 2.5-cm/1-inch cubes and put in a shallow dish. Combine the marinade ingredients and pour over the beef. Leave to marinate for 30 minutes.

2 Heat a wok over a medium–high heat, then add the oil. Add the garlic, ginger and chilli flakes and cook for 30 seconds. Stir in the yellow peppers and baby corn, and stir-fry for 2 minutes. Add the mangetout and cook for a further minute.

3 Remove the vegetables from the wok. Add the beef and marinade to the wok and stir-fry for 3–4 minutes. Return the vegetables to the wok, mix well and cook until all the ingredients are heated through. Serve immediately.

MEAT

KOREAN STIR-FRIED BEEF

Serves: 4   **Prep: 20 mins,**   **Cook: 10–12 mins**
                  plus marinating

Ingredients

450 g/1 lb flank steak

3 tbsp soy sauce

1½ tsp sugar

¼ tsp pepper

5 tbsp beef stock

1 tsp cornflour

1 garlic clove, crushed

2-cm/¾-inch piece fresh
ginger, very finely chopped

½ –1 fresh green chilli,
deseeded and finely
chopped

1 Savoy cabbage,
about 400 g/14 oz

3 tbsp vegetable oil

8 tbsp ready-made kimchi
or sauerkraut

2 spring onions, green parts
included, sliced into 4-cm/
1½-inch shreds

½ tsp toasted sesame oil

small handful coriander
leaves, roughly chopped,
and 2 tsp sesame seeds,
to garnish

Method

1 Put the steak between two sheets of clingfilm
   and pound with a meat mallet to a thickness of
   5 mm/¼ inch. Slice into thin strips, transfer to a
   bowl and mix in 2 tablespoons of the soy sauce,
   ½ teaspoon of the sugar and the pepper. Leave
   to marinate for 2–4 hours, stirring occasionally.

2 Whisk the remaining soy sauce and sugar with
   the stock and cornflour and set aside. Combine
   the garlic, ginger and chilli. Cut the cabbage
   into quarters and discard the tough central core.
   Slice the leaves crossways into 1-cm/½-inch
   strips. Drain the meat and discard the liquid.

3 Heat half the oil in a preheated wok over a high
   heat, add the beef and stir-fry for 3 minutes, until
   brown. Transfer to a bowl with any juices.

4 Wipe out the wok with kitchen paper. Add the
   remaining oil and heat over a medium–high
   heat, stir in the garlic mixture and sizzle for
   15 seconds. Stir in the cabbage and stir-fry for
   2–3 minutes, or until starting to wilt. Add the
   kimchi and fry for a further 2 minutes.

5 Return the beef and juices to the wok and mix.
   Add the spring onions, then whisk in the stock
   mixture. Stir for 1 minute, until slightly thickened.

6 Sprinkle with the sesame oil, garnish with the
   coriander and sesame seeds. Serve immediately.

MEAT

PORK, FRENCH BEANS, CHILLI & PEANUT STIR-FRY

Serves: 4   **Prep: 15 mins**   **Cook: 12–14 mins**

Ingredients

4 tbsp groundnut oil

225 g/8 oz French beans, topped and tailed and cut into 5-cm/2-inch pieces

2 garlic cloves, finely chopped

2-cm/¾-inch piece fresh ginger, finely chopped

1 large spring onion, green parts included, finely chopped

250 g/9 oz fresh pork mince

1½ tbsp rice wine or dry sherry

1½ tbsp soy sauce

1–1½ tsp Sichuan chilli paste

1 tbsp cornflour

6 tbsp chicken stock

4 tbsp dry roasted peanuts

salt and pepper

2 tbsp chopped coriander, to garnish

Method

1 Add 2 tablespoons of the oil to a preheated wok and heat until very hot. Add the beans and stir-fry over a medium–high heat for 4–5 minutes, until slightly blistered. Remove from the wok with a slotted spoon and drain on kitchen paper.

2 Heat the remaining oil in the wok, then add the garlic, ginger and spring onion. Sizzle for a few seconds, then stir in the pork, breaking up the meat with a wooden spoon.

3 Add the rice wine, soy sauce, chilli paste, and salt and pepper to taste. Stir-fry over a medium–high heat for 3 minutes, until the pork is cooked through and no longer pink.

4 Mix the cornflour to a smooth paste with 2 tablespoons of the stock. Mix with the remaining stock and add to the wok. Add the peanuts and stir-fry for a further 2 minutes.

5 Transfer to warmed serving bowls, sprinkle with coriander and serve immediately.

MEAT

BEEF CHOP SUEY

Serves: 4

Prep: 15 mins, plus marinating

Cook: 10 mins

Ingredients

450 g/1 lb ribeye steak

1 head of broccoli, cut into florets

2 tbsp vegetable oil

1 onion, sliced

2 celery sticks, sliced

225 g/8 oz mangetout, sliced lengthways

55 g/2 oz canned bamboo shoots, rinsed and shredded

8 water chestnuts, sliced

225 g/8 oz mushrooms, sliced

1 tbsp oyster sauce

salt

cooked rice, to serve

Marinade

1 tbsp Shaoxing rice wine

½ tsp white pepper

1 tbsp light soy sauce

½ tsp sesame oil

Method

1 Trim any fat from the steak. Slice the meat into thin strips and put in a shallow dish. Combine the marinade ingredients and pour over the beef. Leave to marinate for 30 minutes.

2 Blanch the broccoli in a large pan of boiling water for 30 seconds. Drain and set aside.

3 Heat a wok over a high heat, then add 1 tablespoon of the oil. Add the beef and stir-fry until the colour has changed. Remove from the wok and set aside.

4 Wipe out the wok with kitchen paper. Heat the remaining oil and stir-fry the onion for 1 minute. Add the celery and broccoli and cook for 2 minutes. Add the mangetout, bamboo shoots, water chestnuts and mushrooms and cook for 1 minute. Add the beef and season with the oyster sauce and salt to taste. Transfer to bowls and serve immediately with freshly cooked rice.

MEAT

VIETNAMESE BEEF SALAD

Serves: 2

Prep: 20–25 mins, plus marinating

Cook: 6 mins

Ingredients

1 fresh red chilli, deseeded

2 large garlic cloves

1 tbsp palm sugar

2 tsp soy sauce

juice of 1 lime

400 g/14 oz sirloin steak, thinly sliced

3 tbsp groundnut oil

25 g/1 oz dry-roasted peanuts, roughly chopped

handful fresh mint leaves

handful fresh coriander leaves

Dressing

1 fresh red chilli, deseeded and finely chopped

1 large garlic clove, crushed

1 tbsp palm sugar

2 tbsp Thai fish sauce

juice of 1 lime

½ tsp toasted sesame oil

Salad

½ small head Chinese leaves

2 carrots

6-cm/2½-inch piece cucumber

½ red onion, thinly sliced

Method

1 Put the chilli, garlic, sugar, soy sauce and lime juice into a food processor or blender and process to a thin purée, and pour over the beef. Leave to marinate for 30 minutes.

2 To make the dressing, grind the chilli, garlic and sugar to a smooth paste using a mortar and pestle. Stir in the fish sauce, lime juice and oil.

3 To make the salad, slice the Chinese leaves crossways into wide ribbons. Top, tail and peel the carrots. Slice crossways into 2–3 pieces. Use a swivel vegetable peeler to shave wafer-thin ribbons from each piece, rotating as you shave. Peel alternate strips of skin from the cucumber. Slice in half lengthways and scoop out the seeds. Slice the flesh diagonally into 1-cm/½-inch thick slices. Place into a large salad bowl with the onion. Pour over the dressing and toss to mix.

4 Heat the oil in a wok over a high heat, then add the beef and marinade, and stir-fry for 3 minutes. Pour off the excess liquid and continue to stir-fry for a further 2 minutes, until brown and slightly crisp at the edges. Remove from the wok with a slotted spoon and drain on kitchen paper.

5 Arrange the beef on top of the salad. Add the peanuts, mint and coriander. Toss again and serve while the beef is still warm.

MEAT

STIR-FRIED LAMB WITH ORANGE

Serves: 2 **Prep: 10–15 mins** **Cook: 30 mins**

Ingredients

450 g/1 lb fresh lamb mince

2 garlic cloves, crushed

1 tsp cumin seeds

1 tsp ground coriander

1 red onion, sliced

finely grated rind and juice of 1 orange

2 tbsp soy sauce

1 orange, peeled and segmented

salt and pepper

snipped fresh chives and strips of orange zest, to garnish

Method

1 Heat a wok, without adding any oil. Add the lamb mince and dry-fry for 5 minutes until the lamb is no longer pink. Drain away any excess fat from the wok.

2 Add the garlic, cumin seeds, coriander and red onion to the wok and stir-fry for a further 5 minutes.

3 Stir in the orange rind and juice and the soy sauce, mixing until thoroughly combined. Cover, reduce the heat and leave to simmer, stirring occasionally, for 15 minutes.

4 Remove the lid, increase the heat and add the orange segments. Stir to mix.

5 Season to taste with salt and pepper and heat through for a further 2–3 minutes. Transfer the stir-fry to warmed serving dishes and garnish with snipped chives and strips of orange zest. Serve immediately.

MEAT

BEEF WITH RED PEPPER & LEEKS

Serves: 4

Prep: 20 mins, plus marinating

Cook: 15 mins

Ingredients

450 g/1 lb rump steak

1 garlic clove, crushed

3–4 trimmed young leeks, green parts included, about 300 g/10½ oz total weight

1 thin-skinned red pepper, such as Romano, quartered lengthways, cored and deseeded

3 tbsp groundnut oil

1 tbsp hoisin sauce

1 tbsp soy sauce

6 tbsp beef stock

½ tsp sugar

small bunch of chives, snipped into 2.5-cm/1-inch lengths

salt and pepper

Method

1 Slice the meat into 5-cm x 2.5-cm/2-inch x 1-inch strips and put in a shallow dish. Rub the strips with the garlic, ¼ teaspoon of pepper, and salt to taste. Leave to marinate for 30 minutes or up to 2 hours.

2 Diagonally slice the leeks into 2.5-cm/1-inch pieces. Diagonally slice the red pepper quarters into thin slivers.

3 Preheat a wok over a high heat. Add half the oil and heat until very hot. Add the beef and stir-fry for 2 minutes, until no longer red. Add the hoisin sauce and stir-fry for about 5 minutes, or until the liquid has evaporated and the meat is starting to look sticky. Remove from the wok and keep warm.

4 Wipe out the wok with kitchen paper. Heat over a high heat and add the remaining oil. Add the red pepper and leeks and stir-fry for 2 minutes, until just starting to soften. Add the soy sauce, stock and sugar and stir-fry for 2 minutes.

5 Return the beef to the wok. Season to taste with salt and pepper and stir-fry for a further 1 minute. Stir in the chives and serve immediately.

MEAT

JAPANESE-STYLE PORK

Serves: 2

Prep: 15 mins, plus marinating

Cook: 8 mins

Ingredients

280 g/10 oz pork fillet

2 tbsp groundnut oil

1 garlic clove, thinly sliced

115 g/4 oz French beans, trimmed and sliced into 4-cm/1½-inch lengths

1½ tsp sesame seeds

½ tsp sesame oil

salt and pepper

Marinade

3 tbsp shoyu or tamari (Japanese soy sauce)

3 tbsp mirin

finely grated rind and juice of ½ orange

1 tbsp clear honey

½–1 fresh red chilli, deseeded and finely chopped

1 tsp finely chopped fresh ginger

Method

1 Diagonally slice the pork across the grain very thinly, then cut into thin strips and put in a shallow dish. Combine the marinade ingredients, stirring well to mix in the honey, and pour over the pork. Leave to stand for 1 hour at room temperature, or overnight in the refrigerator. Drain the pork in a sieve set over a bowl, reserving the marinade.

2 Heat a wok over a medium heat, then add the oil. Add the garlic and stir-fry for a few seconds, then add the beans and stir-fry for 1 minute. Add the pork and marinade, and increase the heat to high. Season to taste with salt and pepper, and stir-fry for 4–5 minutes, or until the beans are tender and the pork is cooked through.

3 Sprinkle with the sesame seeds, pour in the sesame oil, then fry for a further 30 seconds. Transfer to a warmed serving dish and serve immediately.

MEAT

RED ROASTED PORK WITH PEPPERED NOODLES

Serves: 2

Prep: 20 mins, plus marinating

Cook: 25–30 mins, plus resting

Ingredients

1 tbsp red curry paste

2 tbsp soy sauce

350 g/12 oz piece pork fillet, trimmed

225 g/8 oz fine dried egg noodles

2 tbsp vegetable oil

1 red onion, chopped

2.5-cm/1-inch piece fresh ginger, peeled and finely chopped

garlic clove, finely chopped

1 orange & 1 red pepper, deseeded and chopped

1 tbsp pepper

1 small bunch of fresh chives, snipped

handful of fresh coriander, chopped

Method

1 Mix together the curry paste and soy sauce in a small bowl and spread over the pork. Cover and leave to marinate in the refrigerator for 1 hour.

2 Meanwhile, preheat the oven to 200°C/400°F/ Gas Mark 6. Place the pork in a roasting tin and roast in the preheated oven for 20–25 minutes until cooked through. Remove from the oven, cover with foil and leave to rest for 15 minutes.

3 Meanwhile, bring a large saucepan of water to the boil, add the noodles and cook for 4 minutes until just tender, or according to the packet instructions. Drain, rinse under cold running water and set aside.

4 Heat the oil in a preheated wok, add the onion, ginger and garlic, and stir-fry over a medium– high heat for 1–2 minutes. Add the orange and red pepper, season with the tablespoon of pepper and stir-fry for 2–3 minutes until tender. Stir in the chives and most of the coriander.

5 Add the drained noodles to the pepper mixture and toss together until well mixed. Divide between two serving dishes. Slice the pork and arrange it on top of the noodles. Scatter with the remaining coriander and serve immediately.

MEAT

STIR-FRIED LAMB WITH MANGETOUT & SPINACH

Serves: 4 **Prep: 10–15 mins** **Cook: 12–15 mins**

Ingredients

4 tbsp groundnut or vegetable oil

550 g/1 lb 4 oz lamb neck fillet, thinly sliced

1 large onion, finely chopped

2 garlic cloves, finely chopped

2 fresh red chillies, deseeded and thinly sliced

175 g/6 oz mangetout

350 g/12 oz spinach leaves, coarse stalks removed

2 tbsp lime juice

3 tbsp oyster sauce

2 tbsp Thai fish sauce

2 tsp caster sugar

5 tbsp chopped fresh mint

salt and pepper

Method

1 Heat a wok over a high heat, then add the oil. Add the lamb and stir-fry for 2–3 minutes, or until browned all over. Remove with a slotted spoon and drain on kitchen paper.

2 Add the onion, garlic and chillies to the wok and stir-fry for 3 minutes. Add the mangetout and stir-fry for 2 minutes, then stir in the spinach and return the lamb to the wok.

3 Add the lime juice, oyster sauce, fish sauce and sugar and cook, stirring constantly, for 4 minutes, or until the lamb is cooked through and tender. Stir in the mint, season to taste with salt and pepper and serve immediately.

MEAT

SICHUAN NUMBING BEEF SALAD

Serves: 4

Prep: 20 mins, plus marinating & cooling

Cook: 10 mins

Ingredients

350 g/12 oz sirloin steak

90 g/3¼ oz egg noodles

1 small red onion, halved and thinly sliced into crescents

6 radishes, sliced

4 good handfuls of peppery leaves such as tatsoi, mustard greens and rocket

1½ tbsp groundnut oil

1 tsp Sichuan pepper, crushed

Marinade

4 tsp Chinese rice wine or dry sherry

½ tbsp soy sauce

4 tsp sugar

2 tbsp hoisin sauce

2.5-cm/1-inch piece fresh ginger, squeezed in a garlic press

Dressing

2 tsp Sichuan pepper, crushed

1½ tbsp light soy sauce

1½ tbsp rice vinegar

2 tbsp cold-pressed sesame oil

Method

1 Trim any fat from the steak. Slice the meat into thin strips and put in a shallow dish. Combine the marinade ingredients and pour over the beef. Leave to marinate for 30 minutes.

2 Cook the noodles in a saucepan of boiling water for 3–4 minutes, or cook according to the packet instructions, until tender. Drain and allow to cool. Snip into shorter lengths. Whisk the dressing ingredients until well blended. Combine the noodles, onion, radishes and salad leaves in a large bowl. Whisk the dressing again and pour two thirds of it over the salad. Toss to distribute the noodles, then divide between individual serving plates.

3 Heat a wok over a medium–high heat, then add the groundnut oil and the Sichuan pepper. Stir for a few seconds to flavour the oil. Add the beef and marinade, and stir-fry for 4–5 minutes until caramelized. Remove with a slotted spoon, and scatter over the salad. Pour over the remaining dressing. Serve immediately.

MEAT

BEEF WITH MISO, CARROTS, CABBAGE & ENOKI MUSHROOMS

Serves: 4

Prep: 20 mins, plus cooling & marinating

Cook: 15–17 mins

Ingredients

2 rump steaks, weighing 450 g/1 lb in total

4 tbsp groundnut oil

2 shallots, chopped

1 large garlic clove, finely chopped

2.5-cm/1-inch piece fresh ginger, finely chopped

2 carrots, sliced into matchsticks

½ green hispi cabbage, halved lengthways and cored, leaves sliced crossways

3 tbsp chicken stock

150 g/5½ oz enoki mushrooms, base removed

1 tsp toasted sesame oil

2 tbsp sesame seeds

small handful coriander leaves, roughly chopped

salt and pepper

Miso sauce

1½ tbsp sugar

4 tbsp mirin

½ tsp wasabi paste

6 tbsp miso

1 tbsp lemon juice

Method

1 To make the sauce, put the sugar and mirin into a small saucepan and heat over a low heat, stirring, until the sugar has dissolved. Add the wasabi paste and miso, and stir until smooth. Remove from the heat, and add the lemon juice. Leave to cool.

2 Put the steaks between two sheets of clingfilm and pound with a meat mallet to a thickness of 5 mm/¼ inch. Slice into 5-cm x 2.5-cm/2-inch x 1-inch strips. Put into a shallow dish and stir in the miso sauce. Cover and leave to marinate in the refrigerator for at least 4 hours or overnight.

3 Drain the beef reserving the excess marinade – there should be about 2 tablespoons.

4 Heat a large wok over a high heat. Add 2 tablespoons of the oil and heat until very hot. Add the beef and stir-fry for 3 minutes until brown. Remove from the wok and keep warm.

5 Wipe out the wok with kitchen paper. Heat over a medium heat, add the remaining 2 tablespoons of oil and heat until very hot. Add the shallots and stir-fry for 2 minutes, until slightly soft. Add the garlic and ginger and sizzle for 15 seconds.

MEAT

6 Stir in the carrots and cabbage. Increase the heat to medium–high and stir in the stock and reserved marinade. Stir-fry for 3 minutes, until just tender. Carefully break up the clump of mushrooms, add to the wok and stir-fry for 30 seconds.

7 Return the meat to the wok and stir-fry for 1 minute to heat through. Season to taste with salt and pepper. Sprinkle over the sesame oil, sesame seeds and coriander and serve immediately.

LAMB WITH BLACK BEAN SAUCE

Serves: 4   **Prep: 20 mins**   **Cook: 13–15 mins**

Ingredients

450 g/1 lb lamb neck fillet or boneless leg of lamb

1 egg white, lightly beaten

4 tbsp cornflour

1 tsp five spice

3 tbsp sunflower oil

1 red onion, sliced

1 red pepper, deseeded and sliced

1 green pepper, deseeded and sliced

1 yellow or orange pepper, deseeded and sliced

5 tbsp black bean sauce

cooked noodles, to serve

Method

1 Using a sharp knife, slice the lamb into very thin strips. Mix together the egg white, cornflour and five spice. Toss the lamb strips in the mixture until evenly coated.

2 Heat a wok over a high heat, then add the oil. Stir-fry the lamb for 5 minutes, or until it crispens around the edges.

3 Add the onion and pepper slices to the wok and stir-fry for 5–6 minutes, or until the vegetables just begin to soften.

4 Stir the black bean sauce into the mixture in the wok and heat through.

5 Transfer the lamb and sauce to warmed serving dishes and serve with freshly cooked noodles.

MEAT

PORK & NOODLES IN PLUM SAUCE

Serves: 4   **Prep: 15 mins**   **Cook: 10–12 mins**

Ingredients

600 g/1 lb 5 oz pork fillet

2 tbsp groundnut oil

1 orange pepper, deseeded and sliced

1 bunch spring onions, sliced

250 g/9 oz oyster mushrooms, sliced

300 g/10½ oz fresh beansprouts

2 tbsp dry sherry

150 ml/5 fl oz plum sauce

250 g/9 oz medium egg noodles

salt and pepper

chopped fresh coriander, to garnish

Method

1 Slice the pork into long, thin strips. Heat a wok over a medium–high heat, then add the oil. Add the pork strips and stir-fry for 2–3 minutes until cooked through.

2 Add the orange pepper and stir-fry for 2 minutes, then add the spring onions, mushrooms and beansprouts.

3 Stir-fry for 2–3 minutes, then add the sherry and plum sauce and heat until boiling. Season well with salt and pepper.

4 Meanwhile, cook the noodles in a saucepan of lightly salted boiling water for 4 minutes, or according to packet instructions, until tender.

5 Drain the noodles, then add to the wok and toss well. Serve immediately garnished with fresh coriander.

★ Variation

Add some thickly sliced pak choi in step 2 for an additional tender taste.

POULTRY

CHICKEN WITH PISTACHIO NUTS

Serves: 4   **Prep: 15 mins**   **Cook: 13–17 mins**

Ingredients

450 g/1 lb chicken breasts, skinned and cut into strips

2 tbsp groundnut or vegetable oil

450 g/1 lb mushrooms, thinly sliced

1 head of broccoli, cut into florets

150 g/5½ oz beansprouts

100 g/3½ oz canned water chestnuts, drained and thinly sliced

175 g/6 oz pistachio nuts, plus extra to garnish

cooked rice, to serve

Marinade

1 egg white, beaten

½ tsp salt

2 tbsp groundnut or vegetable oil

2 tsp cornflour

Sauce

50 ml/2 fl oz chicken stock

2 tbsp soy sauce

2 tbsp dry sherry

1 tsp cornflour

Method

1 To make the sauce, combine the chicken stock, soy sauce and sherry with 1 teaspoon of cornflour. Stir well and set aside.

2 To make the marinade, combine the egg white, salt, oil and cornflour. Toss and coat the chicken in the mixture.

3 In a preheated wok, heat the oil until hot. Add the chicken in batches and stir-fry until golden. Remove from the wok, drain on kitchen paper and set aside to keep warm.

4 Add more oil to the wok if needed and stir-fry the mushrooms, then add the broccoli and cook for 2–3 minutes.

5 Return the chicken to the wok and add the beansprouts, water chestnuts and pistachio nuts. Stir-fry until all the ingredients are heated through. Add the sauce and cook, stirring constantly until thickened. Serve immediately over freshly cooked rice, garnished with pistachios.

★ Variation

When in season aspargus makes a great alternative to broccoli in step 4.

CHICKEN CHOW MEIN

Serves: 4   **Prep: 15 mins**   **Cook: 15 mins**

Ingredients

250 g/9 oz dried medium
Chinese egg noodles

2 tbsp sunflower oil

280 g/10 oz cooked
chicken breasts, shredded

1 garlic clove, finely
chopped

1 red pepper, thinly sliced

100 g/3½ oz shiitake
mushrooms, sliced

6 spring onions, sliced

100 g/3½ oz beansprouts

3 tbsp soy sauce

1 tbsp sesame oil

Method

1 Place the noodles in a large bowl and break
them up slightly. Pour enough boiling water
over the noodles to cover and set aside while
preparing the other ingredients.

2 In a preheated wok, heat the oil over a medium
heat. Add the shredded chicken, garlic,
red pepper, mushrooms, spring onions and
beansprouts to the wok and stir-fry for about
5 minutes.

3 Drain the noodles thoroughly, then add them
to the wok, toss well and stir-fry for a further
5 minutes. Drizzle over the soy sauce and sesame
oil and toss until thoroughly combined. Transfer to
serving bowls and serve immediately.

POULTRY

FIVE-SPICE CHICKEN STIR-FRY

Serves: 4　　　**Prep: 15 mins**　　　**Cook: 8 mins**

Ingredients

300 g/10½ oz
fresh beansprouts

100 g/3½ oz baby corn

4 skinless, boneless
chicken breasts

2 tbsp sesame oil

1 garlic clove, chopped

3 spring onions, sliced,
plus extra to garnish

1 tbsp cornflour

2 tbsp rice wine

1 tbsp five spice

1 tbsp grated fresh ginger

125 ml/4 fl oz chicken stock

Method

1　Wash and dry the beansprouts, cut the baby corn into thick slices and cut the chicken into strips approximately 1 cm/½ inch thick.

2　Heat a wok over a medium–high heat, then add the oil. Add the garlic and spring onions and cook for 1 minute.

3　In a small bowl, mix together the cornflour and rice wine, then add the mixture to the wok. tir-fry for 1 minute, then add the chicken, five spice, ginger and stock, and cook for a further 4 minutes. Add the baby corn and beansprouts, and cook for a further minute until the chicken is cooked through.

4　Remove from the heat, garnish with spring onions and serve immediately.

DUCK WITH CHILLI JAM & DEEP-FRIED SHALLOTS

Serves: 2–4

Prep: 20 mins, plus marinating

Cook: 15–20 mins

Ingredients

2 Barbary duck breasts, weighing about 500 g/ 1 lb 2 oz in total

2 tbsp light soy sauce

3 tbsp Thai fish sauce

2 tsp groundnut oil

3 garlic cloves, very finely chopped

2-cm/¾-inch piece galangal or fresh ginger, very finely chopped

½–1 small fresh red chilli, deseeded and thinly sliced

3 tbsp chilli jam

6 tbsp chopped fresh coriander

pepper

cooked rice, to serve

Deep-fried shallots

groundnut oil, for deep-frying

125 g/4½ oz shallots, thinly sliced lengthways

Method

1 Slice the duck breasts crossways into thin strips. Place in a shallow bowl in a single layer. Sprinkle with the soy sauce and 2 tablespoons of the fish sauce. Toss to coat, then cover and leave in the refrigerator for 2–24 hours, turning once.

2 To make the deep-fried shallots, heat a large wok over a high heat and add enough oil to come to a depth of 2.5 cm/1 inch. Add the shallots and fry for 8–10 minutes, turning with tongs, until golden. Be careful not to let them burn. Remove with tongs and drain on a tray covered with kitchen paper. The shallots will become crisp as they cool. Pour off the oil (keep for another use) and wipe out the wok.

3 Heat the clean wok over a high heat and add the 2 teaspoons of oil. Add the duck and marinade, garlic, galangal and chilli and stir-fry for 3 minutes.

4 Reduce the heat to medium–high and stir in the chilli jam, the remaining fish sauce and the deep-fried shallots. Season with pepper and stir-fry for 2 minutes, moistening with a little water if necessary, until the sauce is well amalgamated. Sprinkle with the coriander and serve with freshly cooked rice.

POULTRY

LEMON TURKEY WITH SPINACH

Serves: 4

Prep: 20 mins,
plus marinating

Cook: 7–10 mins

Ingredients

450 g/1 lb turkey breast, skinned and cut into strips

1 tbsp vegetable oil

6 spring onions, finely sliced

½ lemon, peeled and thinly sliced

1 garlic clove, finely chopped

300 g/10½ oz spinach, washed, drained and roughly chopped

3 tbsp chopped fresh flat-leaf parsley, plus extra sprigs to garnish

cooked pasta, to serve

lemon slices, to garnish

Marinade

1 tbsp soy sauce

1 tbsp white wine vinegar

1 tsp cornflour

1 tsp finely grated lemon zest

½ tsp finely ground black pepper

Method

1 To make the marinade, put the soy sauce, vinegar, cornflour, lemon zest and pepper in a bowl and mix thoroughly. Add the turkey and stir to coat. Cover with clingfilm and marinate in the refrigerator for 30 minutes.

2 Heat the oil in a large preheated wok, add the turkey and the marinade and cook over a medium heat for 2–3 minutes or until the turkey is opaque and cooked through.

3 Add the spring onions, lemon slivers and garlic and cook for another 2–3 minutes. Stir in the spinach and parsley and cook until the spinach is just wilted.

4 Remove from the heat, spoon over freshly cooked pasta and garnish with sprigs of parsley and lemon slices before serving.

POULTRY

CHICKEN FRIED RICE

Serves: 4 **Prep: 15 mins** **Cook: 20 mins**

Ingredients

½ tbsp sesame oil

6 shallots, quartered

450 g/1 lb cooked
chicken, diced

3 tbsp soy sauce

2 carrots, diced

1 celery stick, diced

1 red pepper, deseeded
and diced

175 g/6 oz fresh peas

100 g/3½ oz canned
sweetcorn, drained

275 g/9¾ oz cooked
long-grain rice

2 large eggs, scrambled

Method

1 Heat the oil in a large frying pan or wok over a
medium heat. Add the shallots and cook until
soft, then add the chicken and 2 tablespoons of
the soy sauce and stir-fry for 5–6 minutes.

2 Stir in the carrots, celery, red pepper, peas and
sweetcorn and stir-fry for a further 5 minutes. Add
the rice and stir thoroughly.

3 Finally, stir in the scrambled eggs and the
remaining soy sauce. Serve immediately.

GINGER CHICKEN WITH NOODLES

Serves: 4   **Prep: 15 mins**   **Cook: 10-12 mins**

Ingredients

2 tbsp vegetable oil or groundnut oil

1 onion, sliced

2 garlic cloves, finely chopped

5-cm/2-inch piece fresh ginger, thinly sliced

2 carrots, thinly sliced

4 skinless, boneless chicken breasts, cut into cubes

300 ml/10 fl oz chicken stock

4 tbsp Thai soy sauce

225 g/8 oz canned bamboo shoots, drained and rinsed

75 g/2¾ oz flat rice noodles

4 chopped spring onions and 4 tbsp chopped fresh coriander, to garnish

Method

1 Heat the oil in a wok and stir-fry the onion, garlic, ginger and carrots for 1–2 minutes until soft. Add the chicken and stir-fry for 3–4 minutes, until the chicken is cooked through and lightly browned.

2 Add the stock, soy sauce and bamboo shoots and gradually bring to the boil. Simmer for 2–3 minutes.

3 Meanwhile, bring a saucepan of water to the boil, add the noodles and soak for 6–8 minutes. Drain well, then garnish with the spring onions and coriander and serve immediately with the chicken stir-fry.

POULTRY

STIR-FRIED TURKEY WITH CRANBERRY GLAZE

Serves: 4   **Prep: 10–15 mins**   **Cook: 10–12 mins**

Ingredients

450g/1 lb boneless turkey breast

2 tbsp sunflower oil

15 g/½ oz stem ginger

50 g/1¾ oz fresh or frozen cranberries

100 g/3½ oz canned chestnuts

4 tbsp cranberry sauce

3 tbsp light soy sauce

salt and pepper

Method

1 Remove any skin from the turkey breast. Using a sharp knife, thinly slice the turkey breast.

2 Heat the oil in a large preheated wok, add the turkey to the wok and stir-fry for 5 minutes, or until cooked through. Drain off the syrup from the stem ginger. Using a sharp knife, chop the ginger finely.

3 Add the ginger and the cranberries to the wok and stir-fry for 2–3 minutes, or until the cranberries have softened.

4 Add the chestnuts, cranberry sauce and soy sauce, season to taste with salt and pepper and allow to bubble for 2–3 minutes.

5 Transfer to warmed serving dishes and serve immediately.

PEPPERED CHICKEN STIR-FRY

Serves: 4

Prep: 15 mins,
plus marinating

Cook: 10 mins

Ingredients

350 g/12 oz skinless,
boneless chicken breasts

2 tsp soy sauce

6 tbsp chicken stock

1 tbsp oyster sauce

4 tbsp groundnut oil

1 tsp finely chopped
fresh ginger

1 large garlic clove,
thinly sliced

4 spring onions, white and
green parts separated,
diagonally sliced into 2-cm/
¾-inch pieces

½ tbsp white
peppercorns, crushed

8 baby corn,
halved diagonally

½ small red pepper,
deseeded and thinly sliced

140 g/5 oz canned water
chestnuts, drained

115 g/4 oz mangetout

Marinade

2 tsp soy sauce

1 tbsp cornflour

1 tbsp Chinese rice wine or
dry sherry

¼ tsp salt

Method

1 Cut the chicken into cubes and put in a dish.
Combine the marinade ingredients and pour
over the chicken. Leave to marinate for at least
15 minutes.

2 Mix the soy sauce with the stock and oyster
sauce, and set aside.

3 Heat a wok over a high heat, then add the oil.
Add the chicken and stir-fry for 3 minutes until
cooked through. Remove from the wok with a
slotted spoon and drain on kitchen paper.

4 Reduce the heat slightly, then add the
ginger, garlic, white spring onion and crushed
peppercorns, and stir for a few seconds. Add
the baby corn, red pepper and water chestnuts.
Stir-fry for 2 minutes, then return the chicken
to the wok. Add the mangetout and the soy
sauce mixture, and stir-fry for 1–2 minutes, until
the sauce is thickened.

5 Sprinkle with the sliced green spring onion and
cook for a few more seconds. Serve immediately.

POULTRY

TURKEY WITH MUSHROOMS & COURGETTE

Serves: 4

Prep: 15–20 mins, plus marinating

Cook: 10–12 mins

Ingredients

450 g/1 lb turkey breast

1 tbsp sesame oil

125 g/4½ oz small mushrooms, halved

1 green pepper, deseeded and cut into strips

1 courgette, thinly sliced

4 spring onions, cut into quarters

115 g/4 oz canned bamboo shoots, drained

115 g/4 oz canned water chestnuts, drained and sliced

lemon wedges and cooked rice, to serve

Marinade

4 tbsp sweet sherry

1 tbsp lemon juice

1 tbsp soy sauce

2 tsp grated fresh ginger

1 garlic clove, crushed

Method

1 Cut the turkey into cubes and put in a shallow dish. Combine the marinade ingredients and pour over the turkey. Leave to marinate for 3–4 hours.

2 Heat a wok over a high heat, then add the oil. Remove the turkey from the marinade with a slotted spoon, reserving the marinade, and stir-fry until browned. Remove the turkey from the wok and set aside.

3 Add the mushrooms, green pepper and courgette to the wok and stir-fry for 3 minutes. Add the spring onions and stir-fry for a further minute. Add the bamboo shoots and water chestnuts to the wok, then add the turkey and half the reserved marinade, discard the rest. Stir over a medium–high heat for a further 2–3 minutes, until the turkey is cooked through and the ingredients are evenly coated.

4 Serve immediately in warmed dishes with lemon wedges for squeezing over and freshly cooked rice.

TURKEY WITH HOISIN SAUCE & CASHEW NUTS

Serves: 4

Prep: 15 mins,
plus marinating

Cook: 6–8 mins

Ingredients

450 g/1 lb turkey steaks

4 tbsp groundnut oil

3 large garlic cloves, thinly sliced

4 spring onions, white and green parts separated, diagonally sliced into 2-cm/¾-inch pieces

1 tbsp Chinese rice wine or dry sherry

3 tbsp hoisin sauce

4 tbsp cashew nuts

Marinade

1 tsp cornflour

1 tbsp Chinese rice wine or dry sherry

¼ tsp white pepper

¼ tsp salt

½ egg white, lightly beaten

2 tsp sesame oil

Method

1 Cut the turkey into cubes and put in a shallow dish. To make the marinade, mix the cornflour and rice wine to a paste. Add the remaining marinade ingredients and pour over the turkey. Leave to marinate for 30 minutes.

2 Heat a wok over a high heat, then add 3 tablespoons of the groundnut oil. Add the garlic and white spring onion, and stir for a few seconds to flavour the oil. Add the turkey and reduce the heat slightly. Stir-fry for 2 minutes, until golden brown, then sprinkle with the rice wine. Transfer to a plate with a slotted spoon.

3 Increase the heat to high and add the remaining groundnut oil. Swirl the oil around the wok, then stir in the hoisin sauce. Return the turkey mixture to the wok and stir-fry for 2–3 minutes, turning to coat, until cooked through.

4 Add the cashew nuts and green spring onion. Transfer to a warmed serving dish and serve immediately.

CHICKEN WITH VEGETABLES & CORIANDER RICE

Serves: 4

Prep: 10–15 mins, plus cooling

Cook: 12–15 mins

Ingredients

3 tbsp vegetable oil

2 red onions, 1 chopped and 1 sliced

2 garlic cloves, chopped

2.5-cm/1-inch piece fresh ginger, peeled and chopped

2 skinless, boneless chicken breasts, cut into strips

115 g/4 oz white mushrooms

400 ml/14 oz coconut milk

55 g/2 oz mangetout

1 tbsp Thai fish sauce

2 tbsp Thai soy sauce

350 g/12 oz rice, cooked and cooled

250 g/8 oz pak choi, torn into large pieces

handful of fresh coriander, chopped

Method

1 Heat 2 tablespoons of the oil in a wok, add the chopped onion, garlic and ginger and sauté together for 1–2 minutes.

2 Add the chicken and mushrooms and cook over a high heat until browned. Add the coconut milk, mangetout, fish sauce and 1 tablespoon of the soy sauce and bring to the boil. Simmer gently for 4–5 minutes until tender.

3 Meanwhile, heat the remaining oil in a separate wok or large frying pan, add the sliced onion and cook until soft but not brown.

4 Add the cooked rice, pak choi and coriander and heat through gently until the leaves have wilted and the rice is hot. Sprinkle over the remaining soy sauce and serve immediately with the chicken.

POULTRY

SHREDDED CHICKEN & MIXED MUSHROOMS

Serves: 4   **Prep: 15 mins**   **Cook: 15–20 mins**

Ingredients

2 tbsp vegetable oil or groundnut oil

2 skinless, boneless chicken breasts

1 red onion, sliced

2 garlic cloves, finely chopped

2.5-cm/1-inch piece fresh ginger, grated

115 g/4 oz baby button mushrooms

115 g/4 oz shiitake mushrooms, halved

115 g/4 oz chestnut mushrooms, sliced

2–3 tbsp green curry paste

2 tbsp Thai soy sauce

4 tbsp chopped fresh parsley

cooked noodles, to serve

Method

1 Heat the oil in a wok, add the chicken and cook on all sides, until lightly browned and cooked through. Remove with a slotted spoon, shred into even-sized pieces and set aside.

2 Pour off any excess oil, then add the onion, garlic and ginger to the wok and stir-fry for 1–2 minutes, until soft. Add the mushrooms and stir-fry for 2–3 minutes, until they start to brown.

3 Add the curry paste, soy sauce and shredded chicken to the wok and stir-fry for 1–2 minutes. Stir in the parsley and serve immediately with freshly cooked noodles.

PAPRIKA TURKEY STRIPS

Serves: 4   **Prep: 15 mins**   **Cook: 8–10 mins**

Ingredients

500 g/1 lb 2 oz turkey
breast steaks

1 tbsp paprika

1 tsp crushed
coriander seeds

½ tsp garlic salt

¼ tsp pepper

2 tbsp olive oil

1 red onion, sliced

3 tbsp chopped
fresh coriander

cooked rice, to serve

Method

1 Cut the turkey into long strips, about 1-cm/
½-inch thick.

2 Put the paprika, coriander seeds, garlic salt and
pepper into a large bowl and mix together. Stir in
1 tablespoon of the oil. Add the turkey strips and
turn to coat evenly in the mixture.

3 Heat the remaining oil in a large frying pan or
wok, add the onion and stir-fry for 1 minute. Add
the turkey strips and stir-fry over a fairly high heat
for 6–8 minutes until cooked through.

4 Sprinkle over the chopped coriander and serve
with freshly cooked rice.

POULTRY

CHICKEN SAN CHOY BAU

Serves: 2   **Prep: 15 mins**   **Cook: 6 mins**

Ingredients

1 tbsp vegetable or groundnut oil

100 g/3½ oz cooked chicken, finely chopped

25 g/1 oz water chestnuts, finely chopped

1 tsp finely chopped Chinese chives

25 g/1 oz pine nuts, lightly toasted

1 tsp salt

½ tsp white pepper

6 lettuce leaves, washed

3 tsp plum sauce, to serve

Method

1 In a preheated wok, heat the oil and stir-fry the chicken for 1 minute. Add the water chestnuts and chives and cook for 2 minutes. Add the pine nuts and cook for 1 minute. Add the salt and pepper and stir.

2 To serve, place a spoonful of the mixture in the centre of each lettuce leaf, then top with the plum sauce and fold the lettuce leaf to make a small roll. Serve immediately.

POULTRY

GINGER CHICKEN WITH SESAME SEEDS

Serves: 4

Prep: 20 mins,
plus marinating & cooling

Cook: 11–14 mins

Ingredients

500 g/1 lb 2 oz chicken
breasts, skinned and cut
into strips

2 tbsp groundnut oil

1 leek, thinly sliced

1 head of broccoli, cut into
small florets

2 carrots, thinly sliced

½ cauliflower,
cut into small florets

1 tsp grated fresh ginger

5 tbsp white wine

2 tbsp sesame seeds

1 tbsp cornflour

1 tbsp water

cooked rice, to serve

Marinade

4 tbsp soy sauce

4 tbsp water

Method

1 To make the marinade, combine the soy sauce
with the water in a medium-sized dish. Toss and
coat the chicken strips in the sauce. Cover the
dish with clingfilm and refrigerate for 1 hour.

2 Remove the chicken from the marinade with a
slotted spoon. Heat the oil in a preheated wok,
and stir-fry the chicken and leek until the chicken
is browned and the leek is beginning to soften.

3 Stir in the vegetables, ginger and wine. Reduce
the heat, cover and simmer for 5 minutes. Place
the sesame seeds on a baking sheet under a hot
grill until lightly toasted. Stir them once to make
sure they toast evenly. Set aside to cool.

4 In a small bowl, combine the cornflour with the
water and whisk until smooth. Gradually add
the liquid to the wok, stirring constantly until
thickened.

5 Pile the stir-fry on to a bed of freshly cooked rice,
top with the toasted sesame seeds and serve
immediately.

TURKEY, BROCCOLI & PAK CHOI STIR-FRY

Serves: 4

Prep: 15 mins,
plus marinating

Cook: 10–12 mins

Ingredients

450 g/1 lb turkey breast, skinned and cut into strips

200 g/7 oz basmati rice

1 tbsp vegetable oil

1 broccoli stalk, cut into florets

2 heads pak choi, washed and separated

1 red pepper, deseeded and thinly sliced

50 ml/2 fl oz chicken stock

salt

Marinade

1 tbsp soy sauce

1 tbsp honey

2 garlic cloves, crushed

Method

1 To make the marinade, combine the ingredients in a medium-sized bowl. Add the turkey and toss to coat. Cover with clingfilm and marinate in the refrigerator for 2 hours.

2 Cook the rice in a saucepan of lightly salted water for 10–12 minutes, until tender. Drain and keep warm.

3 Meanwhile, heat a wok over a medium–high heat, add the oil and heat for 1 minute. Add the turkey and stir-fry for 3 minutes. To check that the meat is cooked through, cut into the middle to check that there are no remaining traces of pink or red. Any juices that run out should be clear and piping hot with visible steam rising.

4 Remove the turkey with a slotted spoon, set aside and keep warm. Add the broccoli, pak choi and red pepper to the wok and stir-fry for 2 minutes.

5 Add the stock and continue to stir-fry for 2 minutes, or until the vegetables are tender but still firm to the bite.

6 Return the turkey to the wok and cook briefly to reheat. Serve immediately with the rice.

SEVEN-SPICE CHICKEN WITH COURGETTES

Serves: 4　　　　**Prep: 15 mins**　　　　**Cook: 10–12 mins**

Ingredients

1 tbsp groundnut oil

1 clove garlic, finely chopped

2.5-cm/1-inch piece fresh ginger, peeled and finely chopped

1 small fresh red chilli, deseeded and finely chopped

350 g/12 oz skinless, boneless chicken breasts, cut into thin strips

1 tbsp seven spice

1 red pepper, deseeded and sliced

1 yellow pepper, deseeded and sliced

2 courgettes, thinly sliced

225 g/8 oz canned bamboo shoots, drained

2 tbsp dry sherry or apple juice

1 tbsp light soy sauce

2 tbsp chopped fresh coriander, plus extra to garnish

salt and pepper

cooked noodles, to serve

Method

1 Heat a wok over a medium–high heat, then add the oil. Add the garlic, ginger and chilli and stir-fry for 30 seconds to release the flavours.

2 Add the chicken and seven spice and stir-fry for about 4 minutes, or until the chicken is golden brown. Add the red pepper, yellow pepper and courgettes and stir-fry for 1–2 minutes, or until slightly soft.

3 Stir in the bamboo shoots and stir-fry for a further 2–3 minutes, or until the chicken is cooked through and tender. Add the sherry and soy sauce, season to taste with salt and pepper and cook for 1–2 minutes.

4 Stir in the coriander and serve immediately with freshly cooked noodles. Garnish with extra coriander.

TURKEY TERIYAKI

Serves: 4

Prep: 20 mins,
plus cooling & marinating

Cook: 10–12 mins

Ingredients

450 g/1 lb turkey steaks, cut into strips

3 tbsp groundnut oil

1 small yellow pepper, deseeded and sliced into thin strips

8 spring onions, green part included, diagonally sliced into 2.5-cm/1-inch pieces

cooked rice, to serve

Teriyaki glaze

5 tbsp shoyu (Japanese soy sauce)

5 tbsp mirin

2 tbsp clear honey

1 tsp finely chopped fresh ginger

Method

1 Mix the teriyaki glaze ingredients in a small saucepan over a medium–low heat. Stir until the honey has melted, then remove from the heat and leave to cool.

2 Put the turkey in a large shallow dish. Pour over the glaze, turning the strips so they are well coated. Leave to marinate for 30 minutes at room temperature, or overnight in the refrigerator.

3 Using a slotted spoon, remove the turkey from the marinade, shaking off the excess liquid. Reserve the marinade.

4 Heat a wok over a medium–high heat, then add the oil. Add the turkey and stir-fry for 2 minutes. Add the yellow pepper and spring onions, and fry for 1 minute. Pour in the reserved marinade. Bring to the boil, then reduce the heat slightly and cook for 3–4 minutes, until the turkey is cooked through.

5 Transfer the turkey and vegetables to a serving dish. Boil the liquid remaining in the wok until syrupy, then pour over the turkey. Serve with freshly cooked rice.

STIR-FRY WITH DUCK & PEAS

Serves: 4–6

Prep: 10–15 mins, plus marinating

Cook: 15 mins

Ingredients

450 g/1 lb skinless, boneless duck breasts

3 tbsp groundnut oil

6 large spring onions, white and green parts separated, diagonally sliced into 2-cm/¾-inch pieces

1 tsp finely chopped fresh ginger

300 g/10½ oz mangetout, halved diagonally

140 g/5 oz shelled peas

3 tbsp whole almonds with skin, halved lengthways

55 g/2 oz fresh beansprouts

cooked noodles, to serve

Marinade

1 tbsp soft light brown sugar

3 tbsp warm water

1–2 fresh red chillies, deseeded and very finely chopped

1 tbsp soy sauce

1 tsp Thai fish sauce

3 tbsp lime juice

Method

1 Combine the marinade ingredients in a bowl, stirring to dissolve the sugar. Slice the duck into bite-sized pieces and add to the marinade. Leave to stand at room temperature for 30 minutes, or overnight in the refrigerator.

2 Heat a wok over a high heat, then add the oil. Add the white spring onion and the ginger and stir-fry for a few seconds. Add the duck and the marinade, and stir-fry for about 5 minutes. When the liquid has reduced slightly, add the mangetout and peas and stir-fry for a further 2–3 minutes.

3 Add the almonds, beansprouts and green spring onion, and stir-fry for a few seconds to heat through. Serve with freshly cooked noodles.

TURKEY STIR-FRY WITH SPICED COFFEE GLAZE

Serves: 4–6

Prep: 15 mins,
plus marinating

Cook: 6–10 mins

Ingredients

400 g/14 oz turkey breast fillet, sliced into thin strips

4 tbsp strong black coffee, cooled

4 tbsp teriyaki sauce

2 tbsp clear honey

2 tbsp rice wine vinegar

2 tsp cornflour

2 tsp sesame oil

6 spring onions, trimmed and sliced

1 red pepper, deseeded and thinly sliced

1 yellow pepper, deseeded and thinly sliced

salt and pepper

cooked egg noodles, to serve

Marinade

1 tsp finely grated fresh ginger

2 garlic cloves, crushed

1 tsp five-spice paste

2 tsp sesame oil

Method

1 To make the marinade, add the ginger, garlic, five-spice paste and oil in a shallow, non-metallic bowl with the turkey and stir well. Cover and leave to marinate at room temperature for 1 hour.

2 Mix together the coffee, teriyaki sauce, honey, vinegar and cornflour in a jug. Cover and set aside.

3 Heat the oil in a large wok until almost smoking. Remove the turkey from the marinade, add to the wok and stir-fry over a high heat for 3–4 minutes, until brown. Add the spring onions, red pepper and yellow pepper and stir-fry for a further 1–2 minutes.

4 Pour in the coffee mixture and continue stir-frying for 1–2 minutes, until the sauce has thickened and coated the turkey and vegetables. Season to taste and serve with freshly cooked noodles.

POULTRY

CHICKEN WITH CASHEW NUTS

Serves: 4

Prep: 15 mins, plus soaking & marinating

Cook: 10 mins

Ingredients

450 g/1 lb boneless chicken meat, cut into bite-sized pieces

3 tbsp light soy sauce

1 tsp Shaoxing rice wine

pinch of sugar

½ tsp salt

3 dried Chinese mushrooms, soaked in warm water for 20 minutes

2 tbsp vegetable or groundnut oil

4 slices of fresh ginger

1 tsp finely chopped garlic

1 red pepper, deseeded and cut into 2.5-cm/ 1-inch squares

85 g/3 oz cashew nuts, toasted

Method

1 Marinate the chicken in 2 tablespoons of the light soy sauce, and the Shaoxing, sugar and salt for at least 20 minutes.

2 Squeeze any excess water from the mushrooms and finely slice, discarding any tough stems. Reserve the soaking water.

3 In a preheated wok, heat 1 tablespoon of the oil. Add the ginger and stir-fry until fragrant. Stir in the chicken and cook for 2 minutes, until it turns brown. Before the chicken is cooked through, remove and set aside.

4 Clean the wok, heat the remaining oil and stir-fry the garlic until fragrant. Add the mushrooms and red pepper and stir-fry for 1 minute.

5 Add about 2 tablespoons of the mushroom soaking water and cook for about 2 minutes until the water has evaporated.

6 Return the chicken to the wok, add the remaining light soy sauce and the cashew nuts and stir-fry for 2 minutes until the chicken is cooked through. Transfer to warmed bowls and serve immediately.

NASI GORENG

Serves: 2 **Prep: 15 mins** **Cook: 15–20 mins**

Ingredients

250 ml/9 fl oz water or chicken stock, plus extra if needed

100 g/3½ oz basmati rice

2 tsp vegetable oil

1 small egg, beaten

100 g/3½ oz turkey steak, cut into thin strips

1 carrot, cut into thin lengths

4 spring onions, chopped

2 garlic cloves, crushed

1 fresh red chilli, deseeded and chopped

100 g/3½ oz cooked peeled prawns

50 g/1¾ oz fresh beansprouts

2 tsp soy sauce

pinch of caster sugar

Method

1 Bring the water to the boil in a saucepan and tip in the rice. Return to the boil, then reduce the heat to a simmer. Cover the pan and cook for 10–15 minutes, until the rice is tender and all the water has been absorbed.

2 Meanwhile, heat 1 teaspoon of the oil in a small heavy-based frying pan and add the beaten egg. Swirl the egg until it covers the base of the pan. Cook until the egg has set and is cooked through, then turn out on to a plate. Cut the omelette into strips.

3 When the rice is nearly cooked, heat a wok over a high heat, then add the remaining oil. Add the turkey and stir-fry for 1 minute. Add the carrot, spring onions, garlic and chilli, and stir-fry for a further 2 minutes.

4 Reduce the heat, add the cooked rice to the wok with the prawns, beansprouts, soy sauce and sugar and stir gently for 1–2 minutes. If the mixture sticks, add a little water or stock. Arrange the omelette strips on top and serve immediately.

POULTRY

CHICKEN & SHIITAKE MUSHROOMS

Serves: 4–6 **Prep: 15 mins** **Cook: 10–12 mins**

Ingredients

2 tbsp vegetable oil

675 g/1 lb 8 oz chicken breast, skinned and cut into 2.5-cm/1-inch chunks

1 tsp grated fresh ginger

3 carrots, thinly sliced

2 onions, thinly sliced

100 g/3½ oz beansprouts

225 g/8 oz fresh shiitake mushrooms, thinly sliced

3 tbsp fresh coriander

cooked rice noodles, to serve

Sauce

175 g/6 oz white sugar

225 ml/8 fl oz soy sauce

1 tsp five spice

225 ml/8 fl oz sweet sherry

Method

1 To make the sauce, combine the sugar, soy sauce, five spice and sweet sherry in a bowl. Mix well and set aside.

2 In a preheated wok, heat the oil over a medium–high heat. Add the chicken and stir-fry for 2 minutes, then add the ginger and fry for 1 minute, stirring constantly. Add the sauce and cook for 2 more minutes.

3 One ingredient at a time, add the carrots, onions, beansprouts, mushrooms and chopped coriander. Stir-fry after each addition.

4 Once the sauce has reduced and is thick, transfer the stir-fry to warmed serving bowls. Serve immediately with freshly cooked rice noodles.

CRISP-FRIED SPICY TURKEY

Serves: 4

Prep: 15–20 mins,
plus marinating

Cook: 6–11 mins

Ingredients

450 g/1 lb turkey steaks

2 tbsp Thai fish sauce

2 tbsp light soy sauce

groundnut oil, for frying

40 g/1½ oz peanuts, roughly chopped

4 tbsp chopped Thai basil and lime wedges, to garnish

cooked noodles garnished with chopped spring onions, to serve

Spice paste

2 tsp coriander seeds

1 tsp cumin seeds

2 tsp white peppercorns

seeds from 3 green cardamom pods

1 tsp sugar

1–2 fresh red chillies, deseeded and finely chopped

2 garlic cloves, finely chopped

Method

1 To make the spice paste, dry-fry the coriander seeds over a medium–high heat, shaking the pan frequently, for 2 minutes until starting to pop. Dry-fry the cumin seeds for 30 seconds until fragrant, taking care not to let them burn. Grind the seeds to a paste with the remaining ingredients, using a mortar and pestle.

2 Pound the turkey steaks with a mallet until they are 5 mm/¼ inch thick. Slice across the grain into 5-mm x 4-cm/¼ x 1½-inch strips, and put in a shallow bowl. Rub the spice paste into the meat. Add the fish sauce and soy sauce, tossing to coat. Leave to marinate at room temperature for 20 minutes.

3 Heat a large wok over a high heat and add enough oil to come to a depth of 2.5 cm/1 inch. Add the turkey and any spice paste from the bowl. Fry for 4 minutes, turning with tongs, until beginning to colour. Add the peanuts and fry for a further minute, or until the turkey is crisp and golden at the edges.

4 Remove with a slotted spoon and drain on kitchen paper. Tip into a warmed serving dish and sprinkle with the basil and garnish with lime wedges. Serve alongside freshly cooked noodles garnished with chopped spring onions.

POULTRY

GINGERED CHICKEN & VEGETABLE SALAD

Serves: 4 **Prep: 20 mins, plus marinating** **Cook: 8–10 mins**

Ingredients

4 skinless, boneless chicken breasts

1 tbsp vegetable or groundnut oil

1 onion, sliced

2 garlic cloves, chopped

115 g/4 oz baby corn, halved

115 g/4 oz mangetout, halved lengthways

1 red pepper, sliced

7.5-cm/3-inch piece cucumber, peeled, deseeded and sliced

4 tbsp Thai soy sauce

1 tbsp jaggery or soft light brown sugar

few Thai basil leaves

175 g/6 oz fine egg noodles

Marinade

4 spring onions, chopped

2.5-cm/1-inch piece fresh ginger, finely chopped

2 garlic cloves, crushed

2 tbsp vegetable or groundnut oil

Method

1 Cut the chicken into large cubes, each about 2.5 cm/1 inch. To make the marinade, mix the spring onions, ginger, garlic and oil together in a shallow dish and add the chicken. Cover and marinate for at least 3 hours. Lift the meat out of the marinade and set the meat aside.

2 Heat the oil in a preheated wok and cook the onion for 1–2 minutes. Add the garlic and the rest of the vegetables, except the cucumber, and cook for 2–3 minutes until just tender. Add the cucumber, half the soy sauce, the sugar and the basil, and mix gently.

3 Soak the noodles for 2–3 minutes, or according to the packet instructions, until tender and drain well. Sprinkle the remaining soy sauce over them and arrange on warmed plates. Top with the cooked vegetables.

4 Add a little more oil to the wok if necessary and cook the chicken over fairly high heat until browned on all sides. Arrange the chicken cubes on top of the salad and serve hot or warm.

SWEET & SOUR CHICKEN

Serves: 4

Prep: 15 mins,
plus marinating

Cook: 15–20 mins

Ingredients

450 g/1 lb lean chicken meat, cubed

5 tbsp vegetable or groundnut oil

½ tsp crushed garlic

½ tsp finely chopped fresh ginger

1 green pepper, roughly chopped

1 onion, roughly chopped

1 carrot, finely sliced

1 tsp sesame oil

1 tbsp finely chopped spring onion

cooked rice, to serve

Marinade

2 tsp light soy sauce

1 tsp Shaoxing rice wine

pinch of white pepper

½ tsp salt

dash of sesame oil

Sauce

8 tbsp rice vinegar

4 tbsp sugar

2 tsp light soy sauce

6 tbsp tomato ketchup

Method

1 To make the marinade, combine all the marinade ingredients in a bowl and marinate the chicken pieces for at least 20 minutes.

2 To prepare the sauce, heat the vinegar in a pan and add the sugar, light soy sauce and tomato ketchup. Stir to dissolve the sugar, then set aside.

3 In a preheated wok, heat 3 tablespoons of the oil and stir-fry the chicken until it starts to turn golden brown. Remove and set aside. Wipe the wok clean.

4 In the clean wok, heat the remaining oil and cook the garlic and ginger until fragrant. Add the vegetables and cook for 2 minutes. Add the chicken and cook for 1 minute. Finally add the sauce and sesame oil, then stir in the spring onion and serve immediately with freshly cooked rice.

FRUITY DUCK STIR-FRY

Serves: 4　　　　**Prep: 15 mins**　　　　**Cook: 25 mins**

Ingredients

4 duck breasts, skinned and cut into thin slices

1 tbsp chilli oil

225 g/8 oz baby onions, peeled

2 garlic cloves, crushed

100 g/3½ oz baby corn

175 g/6 oz canned pineapple chunks

6 spring onions, sliced

100 g/3½ oz beansprouts

2 tbsp plum sauce

Marinade

1 tsp five spice

1 tbsp cornflour

Method

1　To make the marinade, mix the five spice and the cornflour in a bowl. Toss the duck in the mixture until well coated.

2　Heat the oil in a preheated wok. Stir-fry the duck for 10 minutes or until just beginning to crisp around the edges. Remove from the wok and set aside.

3　Add the onions and garlic to the wok and stir-fry for 5 minutes or until softened. Add the baby corn and stir-fry for a further 5 minutes. Add the pineapple, spring onions and beansprouts and stir-fry for 3–4 minutes. Stir in the plum sauce.

4　Return the cooked duck to the wok and toss until well mixed. Transfer to warmed serving dishes and serve immediately.

★ Variation

Replace the canned pineapple chunks with the same amount of kumquats, washed and chopped into small chunks.

FISH & SEAFOOD

STEAMED MUSSELS IN LEMON GRASS BROTH

Serves: 4 **Prep: 20 mins** **Cook: 20 mins**

Ingredients

2 shallots, chopped

2 lemon grass stalks, fibrous outer leaves discarded, stems bashed with the flat of a knife

4 thin slices galangal or fresh ginger

2 garlic cloves, chopped

1 small tomato, chopped

300 ml/10 fl oz dry white wine

900 g/2 lb live mussels, scrubbed and debearded

40 g/1½ oz butter

2 tbsp chopped coriander

salt and pepper

Method

1 Put the shallots, lemon grass, galangal, garlic and tomato in a large covered wok. Pour in the wine, season to taste with salt and pepper and bring to the boil. Reduce the heat slightly and simmer for 5 minutes.

2 Discard any mussels with broken shells and any that refuse to close when tapped. Tip in the mussels, cover and cook for 5 minutes, shaking the wok occasionally, until the mussel shells have opened. Discard any mussels that remain closed.

3 Drain the mussels in a colander set over a bowl. Pour the liquid into a small wok. Simmer over a low heat for a few minutes, then whisk in the butter. Check the seasoning.

4 Divide the mussels between warmed soup bowls. Pour over the liquid, sprinkle with the coriander and serve immediately.

★ Variation

You could replace some of the mussels with mixed frozen seafood. Add to the wok at step 2 and cook with the mussels.

EASY PRAWN STIR-FRY

Serves: 4　　　**Prep: 15 mins**　　　**Cook: 10 mins**

Ingredients

1 tbsp groundnut oil

2 tsp sesame oil

4 spring onions, finely chopped

2 garlic cloves, finely chopped

1 red chilli, deseeded (optional) and finely chopped

1 tbsp grated fresh ginger

500 g/1 lb 2 oz raw tiger prawns, peeled and deveined

200 g/7 oz pak choi, coarsely chopped

2 tbsp teriyaki sauce

cooked egg noodles, to serve

Method

1 Heat a wok over a high heat, add the groundnut oil and sesame oil and swirl around the pan to coat the sides. Add the spring onions, garlic, chilli and ginger, reduce the heat to medium–high and stir-fry for 3 minutes.

2 Add the prawns and stir-fry for a further 3 minutes, then add the pak choi and teriyaki sauce. Cook, stirring constantly, for 2 minutes, until the prawns are tender and everything is lightly coated in the sauce.

3 Serve immediately with freshly cooked egg noodles.

CARAMELIZED TUNA SALAD

Serves: 4   **Prep: 20 mins**   **Cook: 7–10 mins**

Ingredients

175 g/6 oz
fresh beansprouts

10-cm/4-inch piece
of cucumber

20 g/¾ oz
coriander leaves

20 g/¾ oz mint leaves

1 tsp sesame oil, plus a few
drops for drizzling

1 tbsp groundnut oil

450 g/1 lb fresh tuna, cut
into 2.5-cm/1-inch chunks

salt

2 tbsp salted roasted
peanuts, crushed, to garnish

Dressing

2 tsp rapeseed oil

1 tsp finely chopped
fresh ginger

½–1 small red chilli,
deseeded and
finely chopped

4 tbsp light soy sauce

1 tbsp Thai fish sauce

1 tbsp tamarind paste

6 tbsp soft brown sugar

Method

1 To make the dressing, heat a small wok over a high heat. Add the oil and fry the ginger and chilli for a few seconds. Add the soy sauce, fish sauce and tamarind paste. Stir for 30 seconds, then add the sugar and stir until dissolved. Remove the wok from the heat and set aside.

2 Rinse the beansprouts in boiling water and drain. Blot dry with kitchen paper. Peel the cucumber, halve lengthways and scoop out the seeds. Thinly slice the flesh diagonally.

3 Put the beansprouts, cucumber, coriander and mint leaves in a bowl. Season with a pinch of salt and a few drops of toasted sesame oil. Toss to combine, then divide between individual serving plates.

4 Heat a wok over a high heat, then add the sesame and groundnut oil. Quickly stir-fry the tuna, turning with tongs, until coloured on the outside but still slightly red in the middle. Arrange the tuna chunks on top of the salad.

5 Reheat the dressing, thinning with a spoonful of water if necessary, and pour over the tuna. Sprinkle with the crushed peanuts and serve immediately.

CHILLI & BLACK BEAN CRAB WITH PAK CHOI

Serves: 4　　　　**Prep: 25 mins**　　　　**Cook: 15–20 mins**

Ingredients

2 cooked crabs, weighing about 1 kg/2 lb 4 oz each

2 tbsp ready-made black bean and garlic sauce

2.5-cm/1-inch piece fresh ginger, squeezed in a garlic press

1½ tbsp rice wine

¼ tsp salt

1 tbsp cornflour

200 ml/7 fl oz chicken stock

1 tsp palm sugar

½ tbsp ketjap manis

½ tsp black pepper

8 tbsp groundnut oil

2 shallots, finely chopped

2 fresh red chillies, deseeded and very thinly sliced

2 large garlic cloves, very thinly sliced

3–4 heads pak choi, about 300 g/10½ oz in total, stems cut into chunks, leaves sliced into broad ribbons

small handful coriander leaves, roughly chopped

Method

1　Pull the claws and legs from the crabs. Cut the claws in two at the joint nearest the pincers. Crack the claw and leg shells with a hammer, taking care not to crush the flesh. Use a skewer or teaspoon to pick out the meat from the body section, discarding the pointed gills (dead men's fingers), stomach sac and brown sediment.

2　Combine the black bean and garlic sauce, ginger, rice wine and salt. Mix the cornflour with 2 tablespoons of the stock to make a paste. Combine the remaining stock with the sugar, ketjap manis and pepper.

3　Heat a large, covered wok over a high heat. Add 6 tablespoons of the oil and heat until almost smoking. Add the crab pieces and stir-fry for 2–3 minutes, turning with a wooden spoon. Remove from the wok, drain on kitchen paper and keep warm.

4　Reduce the heat to medium. Add the remaining oil, then add the shallots, chillies and garlic and stir-fry for 1–2 minutes, without browning. Stir in the black bean mixture and the stock mixture, and bring to a simmer. Add the cornflour paste and stir for 30 seconds, or until slightly thickened.

5 Add the pak choi stems and stir-fry for 1 minute. Add the pak choi leaves and stir fry for a further 2 minutes, or until the stems are starting to soften and the leaves are slightly wilted.

6 Return the crab to the wok, stirring briefly to mix with the pak choi. Cover and cook for 2–3 minutes, until heated through. Tip the contents of the wok into a large, warmed dish. Sprinkle with the coriander and serve immediately.

EGG-FRIED RICE WITH PRAWNS & PEPPERS

Serves: 4

Prep: 20 mins,
plus cooling

Cook: 30–35 mins

Ingredients

225 g/8 oz jasmine rice

1 tbsp groundnut or
vegetable oil

2 spring onions,
finely chopped

2 eggs, beaten

handful of fresh coriander,
chopped, plus extra sprigs
to garnish

Prawns & peppers

55 g/2 oz creamed
coconut

150 ml/5 fl oz boiling water

4 tbsp groundnut oil or
vegetable oil

2 fresh red chillies,
deseeded and roughly
chopped

6 spring onions,
roughly chopped

350 g/12 oz cooked prawns,
peeled and deveined

juice of ½ lemon

6 fresh Thai basil leaves, torn

1 tbsp Thai fish sauce

1 red pepper, deseeded
and cut into strips

Method

1 Bring a large saucepan of lightly salted water to the boil, add the rice and cook for 12–15 minutes, or until just tender. Rinse under cold water, fluff up with a fork and leave to cool.

2 Add the oil to a preheated wok, add the spring onions followed by the rice and stir-fry for 1–2 minutes. Push the rice to one side of the wok and add the eggs to the opposite side. Cook over a medium heat, stirring constantly, for 2–3 minutes until set. Add the coriander then stir the rice through the cooked eggs. Remove from the heat but keep the rice warm in the wok.

3 For the prawns and peppers, chop the creamed coconut and dissolve in the boiling water. Heat half the oil in a separate preheated wok, add the chillies and spring onions and stir-fry over a medium–high heat for 1–2 minutes until just tender. Add the prawns, coconut mixture, lemon juice, basil and fish sauce and bring gently to the boil, stirring occasionally, to ensure that the prawns are heated through.

4 Heat the remaining oil in a wok, add the red pepper and stir-fry over a high heat for 1–2 minutes until sizzling and lightly browned. Stir into the prawn mixture and serve immediately with the egg-fried rice, garnished with coriander.

FISH & SEAFOOD

SIMPLE STIR-FRIED SCALLOPS

Serves: 4 **Prep: 15 mins** **Cook: 5 mins**

Ingredients

450 g/1 lb scallops

2 tbsp sesame oil

1 tbsp chopped
fresh coriander

1 tbsp chopped
flat-leaf parsley

cooked rice noodles,
to serve

Sauce

2 tbsp lemon juice

2 tbsp soy sauce

1 tbsp honey

1 tbsp minced fresh ginger

1 tbsp Thai fish sauce

1 garlic clove, flattened

Method

1 To make the sauce, combine the lemon juice,
soy sauce, honey, ginger, fish sauce and garlic
in a bowl and stir well to dissolve the honey. Add
the scallops and toss to coat.

2 Heat a wok over a high heat, then add the
oil and heat for 30 seconds. Add the scallops,
with their sauce, and the coriander and parsley
to the wok. Stir constantly, cooking for about
3 minutes or until cooked through. Less cooking
time is required if the scallops are small.

3 Transfer to warmed serving plates and serve
immediately with freshly cooked rice noodles.

FISH & SEAFOOD

MUSSELS FRIED RICE

Serves: 6 **Prep: 20 mins** **Cook: 25–30 mins**

Ingredients

2 tbsp peanut or corn oil

1 large onion, chopped

1 garlic clove, finely chopped

8 large tomatoes, peeled, seeded and chopped

225 g/8 oz paella or risotto rice

about 850 ml/1½ pints fish stock

450 g/1 lb mussels, scrubbed and debearded

400 g/14 oz frozen mixed seafood, thawed

175 g/6 oz petit pois, cooked

2 tbsp chopped fresh parsley, plus extra to garnish

salt and pepper

Method

1 Heat the oil in a preheated wok or large frying pan. Add the onion and fry until just softened. Add the garlic and half the tomatoes and stir together well. Add the rice and stir-fry for 2–3 minutes before adding half the stock and bringing to the boil. Simmer for 12–15 minutes, adding more stock as necessary.

2 Discard any mussels with broken shells and any that refuse to close when tapped. Add the remaining mussels to the wok with the mixed seafood and petit pois. Season to taste with salt and pepper and cook for a further 3–4 minutes, until hot, the mussels have opened and the liquid has been mostly absorbed. Discard any mussels that remain closed.

3 Stir in the remaining tomatoes and the parsley. Taste and adjust the seasoning, adding salt and pepper if needed. Serve immediately, garnished with extra parsley.

FISH & SEAFOOD

PRAWN NOODLE BOWL

Serves: 4   **Prep: 20 mins**   **Cook: 8–10 mins**

Ingredients

200 g/7 oz rice noodles

2 tbsp groundnut oil

85 g/3 oz unsalted peanuts

1 bunch of spring onions, diagonally sliced

2 celery sticks, trimmed and diagonally sliced

1 red pepper, deseeded and thinly sliced

1 fresh bird's eye chilli, sliced

1 lemon grass stalk, crushed

400 ml/14 fl oz fish stock or chicken stock

225 ml/8 fl oz coconut milk

2 tsp Thai fish sauce

350 g/12 oz cooked peeled tiger prawns

salt and pepper

3 tbsp chopped fresh coriander, to garnish

Method

1 Put the noodles into a bowl, cover with boiling water, and leave to stand for 4 minutes until tender. Drain and set aside.

2 Heat a wok over a medium–high heat, then add the oil. Add the peanuts and stir-fry for 1–2 minutes until golden. Lift out with a slotted spoon and set aside.

3 Add the spring onions, celery and red pepper and stir-fry over a high heat for 1–2 minutes.

4 Add the chilli, lemon grass, stock, coconut milk and fish sauce and bring to the boil.

5 Stir in the prawns, then return to the boil, stirring.

6 Season to taste with salt and pepper, then add the noodles.

7 Serve in warmed bowls, sprinkled with coriander and the toasted peanuts.

THAI-STYLE STIR-FRIED MONKFISH WITH BROCCOLI STEMS

Serves: 2   **Prep: 25 mins, plus marinating**   **Cook: 15 mins**

Ingredients

550 g/1 lb 4 oz monkfish tail, fins and membrane removed

1 tsp cornflour

2 tsp Thai fish sauce

grated zest of ½ lime

¼ tsp sugar

pinch of salt

1 large head broccoli

4 tbsp groundnut oil

1 shallot, chopped

½ fresh red chilli, deseeded and very thinly sliced

2 tbsp dry-roasted peanuts, coarsely chopped

small handful of Thai basil leaves, or ordinary basil leaves, shredded

Marinade

2-cm/¾-inch piece fresh ginger, squeezed in a garlic press

juice of ½ lime

¼ tsp salt

2 tsp toasted sesame oil

Method

1 Slice the fish either side of the backbone and cut away the 2 fillets. They should weigh about 400 g/14 oz in total. Slice into 3-cm/1¼-inch chunks and place in a shallow dish.

2 To make the marinade, combine all the ingredients and pour over the fish. Leave to stand for 30 minutes, then drain, reserving the liquid.

3 Mix the cornflour with 1 tablespoon of the reserved fish liquid. Combine the Thai fish sauce, lime zest, sugar and salt.

4 Remove the broccoli florets where they meet the stem. (Reserve the florets for another dish.) Peel the thick central stalk. Very thinly slice the stems and the stalk crossways.

5 Heat a wok over a high heat. Add 2 tablespoons of the oil and heat until almost smoking. Add the fish and stir-fry for 2 minutes until the fish flakes easily with a fork and is opaque. Transfer to a plate and keep warm.

6 Wipe out the wok with kitchen paper. Reduce the heat to medium–high and add the remaining oil. Add the shallot and stir-fry for 1 minute, then add the broccoli slices and chilli. Stir-fry for 5–6 minutes, until the broccoli is just soft. Moisten with a little of the fish liquid if necessary.

FISH & SEAFOOD

7 Add the Thai fish sauce mixture and stir-fry for a few seconds. Stir in the cornflour paste and stir-fry for a few seconds, until slightly thickened.

8 Return the fish to the wok and stir-fry for 30 seconds to heat through. Sprinkle with the peanuts and basil, stir-fry for a few seconds and serve immediately.

FIVE-SPICE TUNA STEAKS WITH PAK CHOI

Serves: 4   **Prep: 15–20 mins**   **Cook: 10–12 mins**

Ingredients

600 g/1 lb 5 oz tuna steaks, cut into 3-cm/1¼-inch chunks

2 tbsp lime juice

1 tbsp toasted sesame oil

2 tbsp five spice

pinch of sea salt flakes

4 tbsp groundnut oil

1 large garlic clove, thinly sliced

1-cm/¼-inch piece fresh ginger, thinly sliced

1 shallot, chopped

4 tbsp chicken stock

1 tsp soy sauce

2 heads pak choi, about 200 g/7 oz in total, stems cut into chunks, leaves sliced into broad ribbons

3 tbsp chopped coriander

salt and pepper

lime wedges, to serve

Method

1 Put the fish into a shallow dish and sprinkle with 1 tablespoon of lime juice and the sesame oil, turning to coat. Add the five spice, rubbing it into the flesh well. Sprinkle with the sea salt flakes, and pepper to taste.

2 Heat a large wok over a high heat. Add 2 tablespoons of the oil and heat until almost smoking. Add the fish and stir-fry for 3–4 minutes, until cooked on the outside but still slightly red in the middle. Transfer to a plate and keep warm.

3 Wipe out the wok with kitchen paper. Reduce the heat to medium–high and add the remaining oil. Add the garlic, ginger and shallot and stir-fry for 1 minute, until slightly soft.

4 Stir in the stock and soy sauce, then add the pak choi stems. Stir-fry for 1 minute, then add the pak choi leaves and stir-fry for a further 2 minutes, or until the stems are tender.

5 Return the fish to the wok and stir-fry briefly until mixed with the pak choi. Stir in the remaining lime juice and the coriander and season to taste with salt and pepper. Serve immediately with lime wedges.

GINGER SQUID & PRAWN STIR-FRY

Serves: 4

Prep: 15–20 mins,
plus marinating

Cook: 8 mins

Ingredients

175 g/6 oz squid, cleaned,
tentacles discarded and
cut into thick rings

250 g/9 oz raw king prawns,
peeled and cut in half
lengthways

2 spring onions, finely sliced

2.5-cm/1-inch piece finely
grated fresh ginger

2 garlic cloves,
finely chopped

2 tbsp fresh lemon juice

2 tbsp Thai sweet chilli
dipping sauce

2 tbsp sunflower oil

200 g/7 oz small head of
broccoli, cut into florets

140 g/5 oz mangetout,
halved diagonally

Method

1 Mix together the squid rings, halved prawns,
spring onion, ginger, garlic, lemon juice, chilli
sauce and half the oil in a bowl. Leave to
marinate for 30 minutes.

2 Heat the remaining oil in a preheated wok
and stir-fry the broccoli for 2 minutes. Add the
mangetout and stir-fry with the broccoli for a
further minute.

3 Add the squid and prawn mixture and cook for
3 minutes until the prawns are pink.

4 Spoon into a warmed dish and serve
immediately.

FRIED FISH WITH PINE NUTS

Serves: 4

Prep: 15–20 mins, plus soaking & standing

Cook: 7–9 mins

Ingredients

½ tsp salt

450 g/1 lb white fish fillets, cut into 2.5-cm/ 1-inch cubes

2 dried Chinese mushrooms, soaked in warm water for 20 minutes

3 tbsp groundnut oil

2.5-cm/1-inch piece of fresh ginger, finely shredded

1 tbsp chopped spring onions

1 red & 1 green pepper, deseeded and cut into 2.5-cm/1-inch squares

25 g/1 oz canned bamboo shoots, rinsed and cut into small cubes

2 tsp Shaoxing rice wine

2 tbsp pine kernels, toasted

Method

1 Sprinkle the salt over the fish and set aside for 20 minutes. Squeeze out any excess water from the mushrooms and finely slice, discarding any tough stems.

2 Heat a wok over a medium–high heat and add 2 tablespoons of the oil. Fry the fish for 3 minutes until it flakes easily with a fork and is opaque. Drain and set aside.

3 Wipe out the wok with kitchen paper. Heat the wok over a medium–high heat and add the remaining oil. Add the ginger. Stir until fragrant, then add the spring onions, peppers, bamboo shoots, mushrooms and rice wine and cook for 1–2 minutes.

4 Finally add the fish and stir to warm through. Sprinkle with the pine kernels and serve.

FISH & SEAFOOD

SCALLOPS IN BLACK BEAN SAUCE

Serves: 4 **Prep: 10–15 mins** **Cook: 5 mins**

Ingredients

2 tbsp vegetable or groundnut oil

1 tsp finely chopped garlic

1 tsp finely chopped fresh ginger

1 tbsp fermented black beans, rinsed and lightly mashed

400 g/14 oz prepared scallops

½ tsp light soy sauce

1 tsp Chinese rice wine

1 tsp sugar

3–4 fresh red bird's eye chillies, finely chopped

1–2 tsp chicken stock

1 tbsp finely chopped spring onion

Method

1 Heat a wok over a medium–high heat and add the oil. Add the garlic and stir, then add the ginger and stir-fry together for about 1 minute, until fragrant. Mix in the black beans, add the scallops and stir-fry for 1 minute. Add the light soy sauce, rice wine, sugar and chillies.

2 Lower the heat and simmer for 2 minutes or until the scallops are cooked through. Then add the stock. Finally add the spring onion, stir and serve.

FISH & SEAFOOD

CLAMS IN BLACK BEAN SAUCE

Serves: 4 **Prep: 15 mins** **Cook: 8 mins**

Ingredients

900 g/2 lb small clams

1 tbsp vegetable or groundnut oil

1 tsp finely chopped fresh ginger

1 tsp finely chopped garlic

1 tbsp fermented black beans, rinsed and roughly chopped

2 tsp Chinese rice wine

1 tbsp finely chopped spring onion

salt

Method

1 Discard any clams with broken shells and any that refuse to close when tapped. Wash the remaining clams thoroughly and leave to soak in clean water until ready to cook.

2 Heat a wok over a medium–high heat and add the oil. Stir-fry the ginger and garlic until fragrant. Add the black beans and cook for 1 minute.

3 Over a high heat, add the clams and rice wine and stir-fry for 2 minutes to mix everything together. Cover and cook for a further 3 minutes, or until the clam shells have opened. Discard any that remain closed. Add the spring onion and season to taste with salt. Serve immediately.

PRAWNS, MANGETOUT & CASHEW NUTS

Serves: 4-6   **Prep: 20 mins**   **Cook: 12-16 mins**

Ingredients

85 g/3 oz dry roasted cashew nuts

3 tbsp groundnut oil

4 spring onions, slivered

2 celery stalks, thinly sliced

3 carrots, thinly sliced

100 g/3½ oz baby corn, halved

175 g/6 oz mushrooms, sliced finely

1 garlic clove, chopped

450 g/1 lb raw prawns, peeled and deveined

1 tsp cornflour

2 tbsp soy sauce

50 ml/2 fl oz chicken stock

225 g/8 oz savoy cabbage, shredded

175 g/6 oz mangetout

Method

1 Heat a wok over a medium heat and add the cashew nuts; toast them until they begin to brown. Remove with a slotted spoon and reserve.

2 Add the oil to the wok and heat. Add the spring onions, celery, carrots and baby corn and cook, stirring occasionally, over a medium–high heat for 3–4 minutes.

3 Add the mushrooms and cook until they become brown. Mix in the garlic and prawns, stirring until the prawns turn pink.

4 Mix the cornflour smoothly with the soy sauce and chicken stock. Add the liquid to the prawn mixture and stir. Then add the savoy cabbage, mangetout and all but a few of the cashew nuts and cook for 2 minutes.

5 Garnish with the reserved cashew nuts and serve.

FISH & SEAFOOD

UDON NOODLE STIR-FRY WITH FISH CAKE & GINGER

Serves: 2　　　**Prep: 20–25 mins**　　　**Cook: 6–8 mins**

Ingredients

2 x 150-g/5½-oz packs ready-to-wok udon noodles

1 leek, shredded

200 g/7 oz beansprouts

8 shiitake mushrooms, finely sliced

2 pieces Japanese fish cake, sliced

12 raw prawns, peeled and deveined

2 eggs, beaten

1 tbsp vegetable oil

2 tbsp shoyu (Japanese soy sauce)

3 tbsp mirin

2 tbsp chopped fresh coriander leaves

chilli oil, to drizzle

2 spring onions, finely sliced, to serve

2 tbsp shredded beni-shoga (red ginger), to serve

Method

1 Rinse the noodles under cold running water to remove any oil and tip into a bowl.

2 Add the leek, beansprouts, mushrooms, fish cake, prawns and eggs to the noodles and mix well to combine.

3 Add the oil to a preheated wok and heat until very hot. Add the noodle mixture and stir-fry until golden, and the prawns have turned pink and are cooked through.

4 Add the shoyu, mirin and coriander and toss together.

5 Divide the noodles between two bowls and drizzle with the chilli oil.

6 Sprinkle with the spring onions and beni-shoga and serve.

INDIAN MONKFISH & OKRA

Serves: 4

Prep: 15 mins,
plus marinating

Cook: 25 mins

Ingredients

750 g/1 lb 10 oz monkfish
fillet, cut into 3-cm/
1¼-inch cubes

250 g/9 oz okra

2 tbsp sunflower oil

1 onion, sliced

1 garlic clove, crushed

2.5-cm/1-inch piece fresh
ginger, sliced

150 ml/5 fl oz coconut milk
or fish stock

2 tsp garam masala

fresh coriander sprigs,
to garnish

4 lime wedges, to serve

Marinade

3 tbsp lemon juice

grated rind of 1 lemon

¼ tsp aniseed

½ tsp salt

½ tsp pepper

Method

1 To make the marinade, mix together the
  ingredients in a bowl. Stir the monkfish into the
  bowl and leave to marinate for 1 hour.

2 Bring a saucepan of water to the boil, add the
  okra and boil for 4–5 minutes. Drain and cut the
  okra into 1-cm/½-inch slices.

3 Heat the oil in a preheated wok, add the onion
  and stir-fry until golden brown. Add the garlic
  and ginger and fry for 1 minute. Add the fish with
  the marinade and stir-fry for 2 minutes.

4 Stir in the okra, coconut milk and the garam
  masala and simmer for 10 minutes. Garnish with
  coriander sprigs and serve with lime wedges.

CHILLI PRAWNS WITH GARLIC NOODLES

Serves: 4   **Prep: 20 mins**   **Cook: 10–12 mins**

Ingredients

200 g/7 oz cooked king or tiger prawns, peeled and deveined

4 tbsp sweet chilli dipping sauce

4 tbsp groundnut or vegetable oil

4 spring onions, chopped

55 g/2 oz mangetout, trimmed and halved diagonally

1 tbsp Thai red curry paste

400 ml/14 fl oz coconut milk

55 g/2 oz canned bamboo shoots, drained and rinsed

55 g/2 oz fresh beansprouts

115 g/4 oz dried medium egg noodles

2 garlic cloves, crushed

handful of fresh coriander, chopped

Method

1 Toss the prawns with the chilli sauce in a bowl. Cover and set aside.

2 Heat half the oil in a preheated wok, add the spring onions and mangetout and stir-fry over a medium–high heat for 2–3 minutes. Add the curry paste and stir well. Pour in the coconut milk and bring gently to the boil, stirring occasionally. Add the bamboo shoots and beansprouts and cook, stirring, for 1 minute. Stir in the prawns and chilli sauce, reduce the heat and simmer for 1–2 minutes until just heated through.

3 Meanwhile, cook the noodles in a saucepan of lightly salted boiling water for 4–5 minutes, or according to the packet instructions, until just tender. Drain and return to the saucepan.

4 Heat the remaining oil in a small non-stick frying pan, add the garlic and stir-fry over a high heat for 30 seconds. Add to the drained noodles with half the coriander and toss together until well mixed. Transfer the garlic noodles to warmed serving bowls, top with the chilli prawn mixture and serve immediately, garnished with the remaining coriander.

SALT & PEPPER SQUID WITH GINGER WISPS

Serves: 2 **Prep: 20 mins** **Cook: 20 mins**

Ingredients

groundnut oil,
for deep-frying

1 large garlic clove, very
thinly sliced

300 g/10½ oz cleaned
squid, sliced into
1-cm/½-inch strips

3 spring onions, green parts
included, sliced diagonally
into 2.5-cm/1-inch lengths

pinch of crushed chilli flakes

2–3 handfuls rocket

Salt & pepper mixture

1 tsp Sichuan peppercorns

1 tsp sea salt flakes

Ginger wisps

250 g/9 oz fresh ginger

groundnut oil,
for deep-frying

Method

1 To make the salt and pepper mixture, combine the peppercorns and salt. Pound to a coarse powder using a mortar and pestle.

2 To make the ginger wisps, peel the ginger and very thinly slice lengthways. Stack the slices and slice lengthways again into thin matchsticks.

3 Heat enough oil for deep-frying in a large wok until it reaches 180–190°C/350–375°F, or until a cube of bread browns in 30 seconds. Add the ginger and fry for 6–7 minutes until golden and crisp. Remove from the wok, using a slotted spoon, and drain on kitchen paper. Sprinkle with a little of the salt and pepper mixture. Set aside and keep warm.

4 Heat oil in a separate work over a medium heat. Add the garlic and fry for 30–60 seconds, until pale golden in colour. Remove with a slotted spoon, drain on kitchen paper and set aside.

5 Increase the heat to high and add the squid, spring onions and chilli flakes. Stir-fry for 2 minutes, until the squid is cooked and the spring onions are just tender but still bright green.

6 Arrange the rocket and a small mound of ginger wisps on individual serving plates. Pile the squid mixture on top, and sprinkle with more of the salt and pepper mixture. Serve immediately.

FISH & SEAFOOD

FIVE-WILLOW FISH

Serves: 4–6   **Prep: 20 mins**   **Cook: 18–20 mins**

Ingredients

1 whole sea bass or similar, weighing 450–675 g/ 1–1 lb 8 oz, gutted

2 tsp salt

6 tbsp vegetable or groundnut oil

2 slices fresh ginger

2 garlic cloves, finely sliced

2 spring onions, roughly chopped

1 green pepper, thinly sliced

1 red pepper, thinly sliced

1 carrot, finely sliced

55 g/2 oz fresh or canned bamboo shoots, drained, rinsed and thinly sliced (if using fresh shoots, boil in water first for 30 minutes)

2 tomatoes, peeled, deseeded and thinly sliced

1 tbsp Shaoxing rice wine

2 tbsp white rice vinegar

1 tbsp light soy sauce

1 tbsp sugar

Method

1 Clean the fish and dry thoroughly. Score the fish on both sides with deep, diagonal cuts. Press ½ teaspoon of the salt into the skin.

2 In a preheated wok, heat 4 tablespoons of the oil and cook the fish for about 4 minutes on each side or until the flesh is soft. Drain, then set aside on a warmed dish and keep warm. Wipe the wok clean.

3 Preheat the clean wok and heat the remaining oil and stir-fry the ginger, garlic and spring onions until fragrant. Toss in the vegetables with the remaining salt and stir rapidly for 2–3 minutes. Add the remaining ingredients and mix well for 2–3 minutes. Pour the sauce over the fish and serve immediately.

SESAME NOODLES WITH PRAWNS

Serves: 2

Prep: 20 mins,
plus cooling

Cook: 8–10 mins

Ingredients

1 tbsp oil

16 raw prawns, peeled and deveined

3 shiitake mushrooms, finely sliced

¼ white or green cabbage, shredded

1 carrot, grated

2 bundles of somen or ramen noodles

6 shiso leaves, shredded

Dressing

3 tbsp oil

1 tbsp sesame seeds, toasted

½ cup Japanese rice vinegar

1 tbsp sugar

1 tbsp usukuchi shoyu (Japanese light soy sauce)

salt, to taste

Method

1 To make the dressing, mix together all of the ingredients in a non metallic bowl.

2 Heat the oil in a preheated wok, add the prawns and cook until pink.

3 Add the mushrooms and stir-fry for 1 minute, then add the cabbage and carrot. Remove from the heat and leave to cool.

4 Cook the noodles according to the packet instructions, then drain.

5 Put the noodles in a bowl and add the prawn mixture, add the dressing and mix well.

6 Sprinkle with the shiso leaves and serve.

SPICY SEAFOOD STEW

Serves: 4 **Prep: 20–25 mins** **Cook: 10 mins**

Ingredients

200 g/7 oz squid, cleaned and tentacles discarded

500 g/1 lb 2 oz firm white fish fillet, preferably monkfish or halibut

1 tbsp corn oil

4 shallots, finely chopped

2 garlic cloves, finely chopped

2 tbsp green curry paste

2 small lemon grass stems, finely chopped

1 tsp shrimp paste

500 ml/16 fl oz coconut milk

200 g/7 oz raw king prawns, peeled and deveined

12 live clams in shells, cleaned

8 fresh basil leaves, finely shredded

fresh basil leaves, to garnish

cooked rice, to serve

Method

1 Using a sharp knife, cut the squid body cavities into thick rings and the white fish into bite-sized chunks.

2 Heat the oil in a large preheated wok. Add the shallots, garlic and curry paste and stir-fry for 1–2 minutes. Add the lemon grass and shrimp paste, then stir in the coconut milk and bring to the boil.

3 Reduce the heat until the liquid is simmering gently, then add the squid, white fish and prawns to the wok and simmer for 2 minutes.

4 Add the clams and simmer for a further minute or until the clams have opened. Discard any clams that remain closed.

5 Sprinkle the shredded basil leaves over the stew. Transfer to serving plates, then garnish with whole basil leaves and serve immediately with freshly cooked rice.

MONKFISH STIR-FRY

Serves: 4 **Prep: 15 mins** **Cook: 5–6 mins**

Ingredients

2 tsp sesame oil

450 g/1 lb monkfish steaks, cut into 2.5-cm/1-inch chunks

1 onion, thinly sliced

3 garlic cloves, finely chopped

1 tsp grated fresh ginger

225 g/8 oz fine tip asparagus

175 g/6 oz mushrooms, thinly sliced

2 tbsp soy sauce

1 tbsp lemon juice

Method

1 Heat the oil in a preheated wok over a medium–high heat. Add the fish, onion, garlic, ginger, asparagus and mushrooms. Stir-fry for 2–3 minutes.

2 Stir in the soy sauce and lemon juice and cook for another minute. Remove from the heat and transfer to warmed serving dishes. Serve immediately.

FISH & SEAFOOD

STIR-FRIED FRESH CRAB WITH GINGER

Serves: 4 **Prep: 15 mins** **Cook: 8–10 mins**

Ingredients

3 tbsp vegetable or groundnut oil

2 large fresh crabs, cleaned, broken into pieces and legs cracked with a cleaver

55 g/2 oz fresh ginger, julienned

100 g/3½ oz spring onions, chopped into 5-cm/2-inch lengths

2 tbsp light soy sauce

1 tsp sugar

pinch of white pepper

Method

1 In a preheated wok, heat 2 tablespoons of the oil and cook the crab over high heat for 3–4 minutes. Remove and set aside. Wipe the wok clean.

2 In the clean wok, heat the remaining oil, then add the ginger and stir until fragrant. Add the spring onions, then stir in the crab pieces.

3 Add the light soy sauce, sugar and pepper. Cover and simmer for 1 minute. Serve immediately.

FISH & SEAFOOD

STIR-FRIED SQUID WITH HOT BLACK BEAN SAUCE

Serves: 4 **Prep: 20 mins** **Cook: 8–10 mins**

Ingredients

750 g/1 lb 10 oz squid, cleaned and tentacles discarded

1 large red pepper, deseeded

115 g/4 oz mangetout

1 head pak choi

1½ tbsp corn oil

1 small fresh red bird's-eye chilli, chopped

1 garlic clove, finely chopped

1 tsp grated fresh ginger

2 spring onions, chopped

Black bean sauce

3 tbsp black bean sauce

1 tbsp Thai fish sauce

1 tbsp rice wine or dry sherry

1 tbsp dark soy sauce

1 tsp soft light brown sugar

1 tsp cornflour

1 tbsp water

Method

1 Cut the squid body cavities into quarters lengthways. Use the tip of a small, sharp knife to score a diamond pattern into the flesh without cutting all the way through. Pat dry with kitchen paper.

2 Cut the red pepper into long, thin slices. Cut the mangetout in half diagonally. Coarsely shred the pak choi.

3 To make the sauce, mix together the black bean sauce, fish sauce, rice wine, soy sauce and sugar in a bowl. Blend the cornflour with the water and stir into the other ingredients in the bowl. Reserve the mixture until required.

4 Heat the oil in a preheated wok. Add the chilli, garlic, ginger and spring onions and stir-fry for 1 minute. Add the red pepper and stir-fry for 2 minutes.

5 Add the squid and stir-fry over a high heat for a further minute. Stir in the mangetout and pak choi and stir for a further minute, or until wilted.

6 Stir in the sauce and cook, stirring constantly, for 2 minutes or until the sauce thickens and clears. Serve immediately.

FISH & SEAFOOD

GINGER PRAWNS WITH OYSTER MUSHROOMS

Serves: 4   **Prep: 10 mins**   **Cook: 12 mins**

Ingredients

3 tbsp vegetable oil

3 carrots, thinly sliced

350 g/12 oz oyster mushrooms, thinly sliced

1 large red pepper, deseeded and thinly sliced

450 g/1 lb raw king prawns, peeled and deveined

2 garlic cloves, crushed

cooked rice, to serve

fresh coriander sprigs, to garnish

Sauce

150 ml/5 fl oz chicken stock

2 tsp sesame seeds

1 tbsp grated fresh ginger

1 tbsp soy sauce

¼ tsp hot pepper sauce

1 tsp cornflour

Method

1 To make the sauce, stir together the stock, sesame seeds, ginger, soy sauce, hot pepper sauce and cornflour until well blended. Set aside.

2 Heat a wok over a medium–high heat, then add 2 tablespoons of oil. Add the carrots and stir-fry for 3 minutes, remove from the wok and set aside.

3 Add the remaining oil to the wok and stir-fry the mushrooms for 2 minutes. Remove from the wok and set aside.

4 Add the red pepper, prawns and garlic to the wok and stir-fry for 3 minutes, until the prawns turn pink and start to curl. Stir the sauce again and pour it into the wok.

5 Cook until the mixture bubbles, then return the carrots and mushrooms to the wok. Cover and cook for a further 2 minutes, until heated through. Serve over freshly cooked rice and garnish with coriander sprigs.

STIR-FRIED RICE NOODLES WITH MARINATED FISH

Serves: 4

Prep: 20 mins, plus marinating

Cook: 6–8 mins

Ingredients

450 g/1 lb monkfish or cod, cubed

225 g/8 oz salmon fillets, cubed

115 g/4 oz thick rice noodles

2 tbsp vegetable or groundnut oil

2 shallots, sliced

2 garlic cloves, finely chopped

1 fresh red chilli, deseeded and chopped

2 tbsp Thai soy sauce

2 tbsp chilli sauce

sprigs of fresh coriander, to garnish

Marinade

2 tbsp vegetable or groundnut oil

2 fresh green chillies, deseeded and chopped

grated rind and juice of 1 lime

1 tbsp fish sauce

Method

1. Combine the marinade ingredients and pour over the fish. Leave to marinate for 2 hours.

2. Prepare the noodles according to the packet instructions. Drain well.

3. Heat a wok over a medium–high heat and add the oil. Sauté the shallots, garlic and red chilli until lightly browned. Add the soy sauce and chilli sauce. Add the fish and the marinade to the wok and stir-fry gently for 2–3 minutes until cooked through.

4. Add the drained noodles and stir gently. Garnish with coriander and serve immediately.

MACKEREL WITH GINGER

Serves: 2–3

Prep: 20 mins,
plus standing

Cook: 8 mins

Ingredients

4 mackerel fillets with skin,
weighing about
450 g/1 lb in total

1 tsp finely chopped fresh
ginger, plus 2.5 cm/1-inch
piece finely shredded
lengthways

½ tsp salt

4 tbsp groundnut oil

2½ tbsp plain flour

3 spring onions, green parts
included, sliced

finely shredded Chinese
leaves, to garnish

Sauce

2 tbsp light soy sauce

½ tsp sugar

2 tsp Chinese rice wine or
dry sherry

Method

1 Slice the mackerel fillets in half crossways.
Diagonally slash the skin of each piece once or
twice. Combine the chopped ginger with the
salt, then rub the mixture over both sides of the
fish, rubbing it into the slashes and any crevices
in the flesh. Leave to stand for 15 minutes.

2 Combine the sauce ingredients in a small bowl
and set aside.

3 Heat a wok over a medium–high heat and add
the oil. Dredge the mackerel fillets in the flour
and add to the wok. Fry for 4 minutes, turning
once. Pour the sauce over the fish, sprinkle with
the shredded ginger and spring onions, and fry
for a further 2 minutes.

4 Transfer to a warmed serving dish and garnish
with a few shreds of Chinese leaves. Serve
immediately.

★ Variation

Try adding ½ teaspoon of crushed fennel seeds
to the chopped ginger. They are particularly
good with mackerel.

FISH & SEAFOOD

VEGETABLES

KALE STIR-FRY

Serves: 4   **Prep: 20–25 mins**   **Cook: 15 mins**

Ingredients

750 g/1 lb 10 oz kale

2 tbsp sunflower oil

1 onion, chopped

4 large garlic cloves, finely chopped

2 red peppers, deseeded and thinly sliced

1 large carrot, coarsely grated

100 g/3½ oz broccoli, cut into very small florets

125 ml/4 fl oz vegetable stock

115 g/4 oz mixed sprouted beans

handful of toasted cashew nuts, chopped

salt and pepper

lemon wedges, to serve

Method

1 Using a sharp knife, cut out the thick central stems from the kale. Stack several leaves on top of each other, then finely shred; repeat until all the kale is shredded. Set aside.

2 Heat a large wok with a lid over a high heat until a splash of water 'dances' on the surface. Add the oil and swirl it around. Add the onion and stir-fry for about 3 minutes, then add the garlic, peppers and carrot and continue stir-frying until the onion is tender and the peppers are starting to soften.

3 Add the broccoli and the kale to the wok and stir. Add the stock and salt and pepper to taste, reduce the heat to medium, cover and simmer for about 5 minutes, until the kale is tender.

4 Remove the lid and allow any excess liquid to evaporate. Use 2 forks to mix the sprouted beans through the other ingredients, then adjust the seasoning, adding salt and pepper if needed.

5 Transfer to serving plates, scatter over the nuts and serve with lemon wedges.

★ Variation

For a bit of a kick add a pinch of dried chilli flakes when adding the broccoli in step 3.

VEGETABLES

STIR-FRIED TOFU WITH BEANSPROUTS

Serves: 4 **Prep: 15 mins** **Cook: 20 mins**

Ingredients

1½ tbsp light soy sauce

1 tbsp oyster sauce

2 tbsp chicken stock

groundnut oil, for deep-frying

350 g/12 oz firm tofu, cubed

2 large garlic cloves, thinly sliced

115 g/4 oz mangetout, trimmed and halved diagonally

4 spring onions, sliced diagonally into 2.5-cm/1-inch pieces

115 g/4 oz beansprouts

salt and pepper

½ bunch garlic chives or ordinary chives, snipped into 2.5-cm/1-inch lengths, to garnish

few drops of sesame oil, to garnish

Method

1 Combine the soy sauce, oyster sauce and chicken stock in a small bowl and set aside.

2 Heat enough oil for deep-frying in a large wok until it reaches 180–190°C/350–375°F, or until a cube of bread browns in 30 seconds. Add the tofu and fry for 5–7 minutes until golden brown, turning with tongs. Remove with a slotted spoon and drain on kitchen paper. Season with salt and pepper.

3 Pour the oil from the wok, reserving 1 tablespoon, and wipe out the wok with kitchen paper. Heat the reserved oil in the wok, add the garlic and stir-fry for a few seconds to flavour the oil. Add the mangetout and spring onions, and stir-fry for 2 minutes.

4 Add the beansprouts and soy sauce mixture. Stir-fry for 1 minute, then toss in the fried tofu and stir to mix. Sprinkle with the chives and a few drops of sesame oil, and serve immediately.

CRISPY NOODLES WITH PAK CHOI IN OYSTER SAUCE

Serves: 4 **Prep: 15 mins** **Cook: 18–20 mins**

Ingredients

groundnut oil, for deep-frying

100 g/3½ oz dried rice vermicelli noodles

1 tbsp crushed palm sugar or muscovado sugar

1 tbsp rice vinegar

1 tbsp fish sauce

1 tbsp lime juice

6 spring onions, sliced

1 garlic clove, thinly sliced

350 g/12 oz small pak choi, quartered lengthways

3 tbsp oyster sauce

sesame seeds, to sprinkle

Method

1 Heat a deep pan of oil until a piece of noodle sizzles instantly. Add the noodles and fry in batches for 15–20 seconds, until puffed and golden. Drain on kitchen paper.

2 Heat the sugar, vinegar, fish sauce and lime juice in a small pan, until the sugar dissolves. Boil for 20–30 seconds until syrupy.

3 Heat 2 tablespoons of the oil in a wok and stir-fry the spring onions and garlic for 1 minute. Add the pak choi and stir-fry for 2–3 minutes. Stir in the oyster sauce.

4 Toss the noodles with the syrup and transfer to individual serving bowls with the pak choi.

5 Serve the dish immediately, sprinkled with sesame seeds.

STIR-FRIED RICE WITH GREEN VEGETABLES

Serves: 4

Prep: 10–15 mins,
plus cooling & chilling

Cook: 20–25 mins

Ingredients

225 g/8 oz jasmine rice

2 tbsp vegetable or groundnut oil

1 tbsp green curry paste

6 spring onions, sliced

2 garlic cloves, crushed

1 courgette, cut into thin sticks

115 g/4 oz French beans

175 g/6 oz asparagus, trimmed

3–4 fresh Thai basil leaves

salt

Method

1 Cook the rice in lightly salted boiling water for 12–15 minutes, drain well, then cool thoroughly and chill.

2 Heat the oil in a wok and stir-fry the curry paste for 1 minute. Add the spring onions and garlic and stir-fry for 1 minute.

3 Add the courgette, beans and asparagus and stir-fry for 3–4 minutes, until just tender. Break up the rice and add it to the wok. Cook, stirring constantly for 2–3 minutes, until the rice is hot. Stir in the basil and serve immediately.

TOFU & VEGETABLE SALAD

Serves: 4   **Prep: 20 mins**   **Cook: 10–15 mins**

Ingredients

4 tbsp vegetable or groundnut oil

225 g/8 oz tofu with herbs, cubed

1 red onion, sliced

4 spring onions, cut into 5-cm/2-inch lengths

1 garlic clove, chopped

2 carrots, cut into matchsticks

115 g/4 oz fine French beans, trimmed

1 yellow pepper, cut into strips

115 g/4 oz broccoli, cut into florets

1 large courgette, cut into matchsticks

55 g/2 oz beansprouts

2 tbsp Thai red curry paste

4 tbsp Thai soy sauce

1 tbsp rice wine vinegar

1 tsp palm sugar or soft light brown sugar

a few Thai basil leaves, plus extra to garnish

350 g/12 oz rice vermicelli noodles

Method

1 Heat the oil in a preheated wok and fry the tofu cubes for 3–4 minutes until browned on all sides. Lift out of the oil and drain on kitchen paper.

2 Add the red onion, spring onions, garlic and carrots to the hot oil and fry for 1–2 minutes before adding the rest of the vegetables, except for the beansprouts. Stir-fry for 2–3 minutes. Add the beansprouts, then stir in the curry paste, soy sauce, vinegar, sugar and basil leaves. Cook for 30 seconds.

3 Soak the noodles in boiling water or stock for 2–3 minutes, or according to the packet instructions, until tender, and drain well. Arrange the freshly cooked noodles in warmed bowls.

4 Pile the vegetables over the noodles, and garnish with extra basil, and serve topped with the tofu cubes.

VEGETABLES

OYSTER MUSHROOMS WITH PEANUT CHILLI SAUCE

Serves: 4   **Prep: 10–15 mins**   **Cook: 8–10 mins**

Ingredients

1 tbsp vegetable or groundnut oil

4 spring onions, finely sliced

1 carrot, cut into thin strips

1 courgette, cut into thin strips

½ head of broccoli, cut into florets

450 g/1 lb oyster mushrooms, thinly sliced

2 tbsp crunchy peanut butter

1 tsp chilli powder, or to taste

3 tbsp water

cooked rice, to serve

lime wedges, to serve

Method

1 Heat the oil in a preheated wok until almost smoking. Stir-fry the spring onions for 1 minute. Add the carrot and courgette and stir-fry for another minute. Then add the broccoli and cook for 1 more minute.

2 Stir in the mushrooms and cook until they are soft and at least half the liquid they produce has evaporated. Add the peanut butter and stir well. Season with the chilli powder to taste. Finally add the water and cook for 1 more minute.

3 Serve over freshly cooked rice with wedges of lime.

VEGETABLES

SPICY VEGETARIAN STIR-FRY

Serves: 4 **Prep: 15 mins** **Cook: 20 mins**

Ingredients

3 tbsp vegetable oil

½ tsp turmeric

225 g/8 oz potatoes, cut into 1-cm/½-inch cubes

3 shallots, finely chopped

1 bay leaf

½ tsp ground cumin

1 tsp finely grated fresh ginger

¼ tsp chilli powder

4 tomatoes, roughly chopped

300 g/10½ oz spinach, de-stalked & chopped

125 g/4½ oz peas

1 tbsp lemon juice

salt and pepper

cooked basmati rice, to serve

Method

1 In a preheated wok, heat 2 tablespoons of the oil and add the turmeric and a pinch of salt. Carefully add the potatoes, stirring constantly to coat in the turmeric. Stir-fry for 5 minutes, then remove from the wok and set aside.

2 Heat the remaining tablespoon of oil and stir-fry the shallots for 1–2 minutes. Mix in the bay leaf, cumin, ginger and chilli powder, then add the tomatoes and stir-fry for 2 minutes.

3 Add the spinach, mixing well to combine all the flavours. Cover and simmer for 2–3 minutes. Return the potatoes to the wok and add the peas and lemon juice. Cook for 5 minutes, or until the potatoes are tender.

4 Remove the wok from the heat and discard the bay leaf, then season with salt and pepper. Serve with freshly cooked basmati rice.

VEGETABLES

MIXED VEGETABLES WITH BASIL

Serves: 4   **Prep: 15–20 mins**   **Cook: 7–10 mins**

Ingredients

2 tbsp vegetable or groundnut oil, plus extra for shallow frying

2 garlic cloves, chopped

1 onion, sliced

115 g/4 oz baby corn, cut in half diagonally

½ cucumber, peeled, halved, deseeded and sliced

225 g/8 oz canned water chestnuts, drained and rinsed

55 g/2 oz mangetout

115 g/4 oz shiitake mushrooms, halved

1 red pepper, deseeded and thinly sliced

1 tbsp soft light brown sugar

2 tbsp Thai soy sauce

1 tbsp Thai fish sauce

1 tbsp rice vinegar

8–12 fresh Thai basil sprigs

cooked rice, to serve

Method

1 Heat a wok over a high heat, then add the oil. Add the garlic and onion and stir-fry for 1–2 minutes. Add the baby corn, cucumber, water chestnuts, mangetout, mushrooms and red pepper and stir-fry for 2–3 minutes, until starting to soften.

2 Add the sugar, soy sauce, fish sauce and vinegar and gradually bring to the boil. Simmer for 1–2 minutes.

3 Meanwhile, heat enough oil for shallow frying in a wok and, when hot, add the basil sprigs. Cook for 20–30 seconds until crisp. Remove with a slotted spoon and drain on kitchen paper.

4 Garnish the vegetable stir-fry with the crispy basil and serve immediately with freshly cooked rice.

LEAFY GREENS, LEEK & ASPARAGUS STIR-FRY

Serves: 4–6   **Prep: 15–20 mins**   **Cook: 10 mins**

Ingredients

500 g/1 lb 2 oz mixed leafy greens, such as pak choi, cavolo nero, chard and spinach

225 g/8 oz asparagus

5 tbsp groundnut oil

3-cm/1¼-inch piece fresh ginger, diced

½–1 fresh green or red chilli, deseeded and diced

3 large garlic cloves, peeled and thinly sliced

6 baby leeks, lower green part included, sliced into rounds

3–4 tbsp vegetable stock or water

2 tbsp soy sauce

½ tsp salt

small handful fresh coriander leaves

1 tsp sesame seeds

1 tbsp toasted sesame oil

pepper

cooked rice, to serve

Method

1 Cut away the stalks and large central ribs from the greens. Slice the stalks into 1-cm/½-inch pieces. Stack the leaves and slice into ribbons.

2 Snap off the woody ends from the asparagus and discard. Chop the stems into 2-cm/¾-inch pieces. Leave the tips whole.

3 Heat a large wok over a high heat and add the oil. When almost smoking, add the ginger, chilli and garlic. Stir-fry for 30 seconds.

4 Add the leeks, asparagus and the chopped stalks from the greens. Add stock to moisten and stir-fry for a further 2 minutes.

5 Add the sliced leaves, soy sauce, salt and a little pepper and stir-fry for 3 minutes.

6 Stir in the coriander, sesame seeds and sesame oil and stir-fry for 30 seconds. Serve immediately with freshly cooked rice.

SICHUAN NOODLES

Serves: 4　　　**Prep: 15 mins**　　　**Cook: 10–12 mins**

Ingredients

250 g/9 oz thick egg noodles

2 tbsp peanut or corn oil

2 large garlic cloves, very finely chopped

1 large red onion, cut in half and thinly sliced

125 ml/4 fl oz vegetable stock or water

2 tbsp bottled chilli bean sauce

2 tbsp Chinese sesame paste

1 tbsp dried Sichuan peppercorns, roasted and ground

1 tsp light soy sauce

2 small pak choi or other Chinese cabbage, cut into quarters

1 large carrot, grated

Method

1 Cook the noodles in a saucepan of boiling water for 4 minutes, or according to the packet instructions, until soft. Drain and rinse with cold water and set aside.

2 Heat a wok over high heat and add the oil. Add the garlic and onion and stir-fry for 1 minute. Add the vegetable stock, chilli bean sauce, sesame paste, ground Sichuan peppercorns and soy sauce and bring to the boil, stirring to blend the ingredients together.

3 Add the pak choi quarters and grated carrot and continue to stir-fry for 1–2 minutes, until they are just wilted.

4 Add the noodles and continue stir-frying, using 2 forks, mix all the ingredients together until the noodles are hot.

5 Transfer to bowls and serve.

SWEET & SOUR TOFU WITH VEGETABLES

Serves: 4　　　**Prep: 15 mins**　　　**Cook: 10–12 mins**

Ingredients

2 tbsp vegetable oil

2 garlic cloves, crushed

2 celery stalks, thinly sliced

1 carrot, cut into thin strips

1 green pepper, diced

85 g/3 oz mangetout, cut in half diagonally

8 baby corn

115 g/4 oz beansprouts

450 g/1 lb firm tofu, rinsed, drained and cut into cubes

Sauce

2 tbsp light brown sugar

2 tbsp wine vinegar

225 ml/8 fl oz vegetable stock

1 tsp tomato purée

1 tbsp cornflour

Method

1 Heat the oil in a preheated wok until it is almost smoking. Reduce the heat slightly, add the garlic, celery, carrot, pepper, mangetout and baby corn and stir-fry for 3–4 minutes.

2 Add the beansprouts and tofu to the wok and cook for 2 minutes, stirring frequently.

3 To make the sauce, mix the sugar, wine vinegar, stock, tomato purée and cornflour, stirring well to mix. Stir into the wok, bring to the boil and cook, stirring constantly, until the sauce thickens. Continue to cook for 1 minute. Serve immediately.

BROCCOLI WITH PEANUTS

Serves: 4   **Prep: 15 mins**   **Cook: 8–10 mins**

Ingredients

3 tbsp vegetable or groundnut oil

1 lemon grass stem, roughly chopped

2 fresh red chillies, deseeded and chopped

2.5-cm/1-inch piece fresh ginger, grated

3 kaffir lime leaves, roughly torn

3 tbsp Thai green curry paste

1 onion, chopped

1 red pepper, deseeded and chopped

350 g/12 oz broccoli, cut into florets

115 g/4 oz French beans

55 g/2 oz unsalted peanuts

Method

1 Put 2 tablespoons of the oil, the lemon grass, chillies, ginger, lime leaves and curry paste into a food processor or blender and process to a paste.

2 Heat a wok over a medium heat and add the remaining oil. Add the spice paste, onion and red pepper and stir-fry for 2–3 minutes, until the vegetables start to soften. Add the broccoli and French beans, cover and cook over a low heat, stirring occasionally, for 4–5 minutes, until tender.

3 Meanwhile, toast or dry-fry the peanuts until lightly browned. Add them to the broccoli mixture and toss together. Serve immediately.

VEGETABLES

AUBERGINE WITH RED PEPPERS

Serves: 4

Prep: 10–15 mins

Cook: 10 mins,
plus resting

Ingredients

3 tbsp vegetable or groundnut oil

1 garlic clove, finely chopped

3 aubergines, halved lengthways and cut diagonally into 2.5-cm/1-inch pieces

1 tsp white rice vinegar

1 red pepper, deseeded and finely sliced

2 tbsp light soy sauce

1 tsp sugar

1 tbsp finely chopped coriander leaves, to garnish

Method

1 Heat a wok over a high heat, then add the oil and heat until it begins to smoke. Add in the garlic, stir-fry until fragrant, then add the aubergines. Stir-fry for 30 seconds, then add the vinegar. Reduce the heat and cook, covered, for 5 minutes, stirring from time to time.

2 When the aubergine pieces are soft, add the pepper and stir. Add the soy sauce and sugar and cook, uncovered, for 2 minutes.

3 Remove the wok from the heat and leave to rest for 2 minutes. Transfer to a serving dish, garnish with coriander and serve.

VEGETABLES

CARROT & ORANGE STIR-FRY

Serves: 4   **Prep: 15 mins**   **Cook: 10 mins**

Ingredients

2 tbsp sunflower oil

450 g/1 lb carrots, grated

225 g/8 oz leeks, shredded

2 oranges, peeled and segmented

2 tbsp tomato ketchup

1 tbsp demerara sugar

2 tbsp light soy sauce

100 g/3½ oz peanuts, chopped

Method

1 Heat the oil in a large wok. Add the carrots and leeks to the wok and stir-fry for 2–3 minutes, or until the vegetables are just soft.

2 Add the oranges to the wok and heat through gently, ensuring that you do not break up the orange segments as you stir the mixture.

3 Mix together the ketchup, sugar and soy sauce in a small bowl.

4 Add the ketchup mixture to the wok and stir-fry for a further 2 minutes.

5 Transfer the stir-fry to warmed serving bowls and scatter over the peanuts. Serve immediately.

VEGETABLES

STIR-FRIED JAPANESE NOODLES

Serves: 4

Prep: 15 mins,
plus soaking

Cook: 10–12 mins

Ingredients

225 g/8 oz Japanese egg
noodles

2 tbsp sunflower oil

1 red onion, sliced

1 garlic clove, crushed

500 g/1 lb 2 oz mixed
mushrooms such as shiitake,
oyster and brown cap

350 g/12 oz pak choi

2 tbsp sweet sherry

6 tbsp soy sauce

4 spring onions, trimmed
and sliced, to garnish

1 tbsp sesame seeds,
toasted, to garnish

Method

1 Place the noodles in a large bowl, pour over enough boiling water to cover and leave to soak for 10 minutes.

2 Heat the oil in a large preheated wok. Add the red onion and garlic to the wok and stir-fry for 2–3 minutes or until softened. Add the mushrooms to the wok and stir-fry for 5 minutes or until softened. Drain the noodles and add to the wok.

3 Add the pak choi, sweet sherry and soy sauce to the wok and toss to mix well. Stir-fry for 2–3 minutes or until the liquid is just bubbling. Transfer the noodle mixture to warmed serving bowls, garnish with sliced spring onions and toasted sesame seeds and serve immediately.

VEGETABLES

PAK CHOI WITH RED ONIONS & CASHEW NUTS

Serves: 4   **Prep: 15 mins**   **Cook: 15 mins**

Ingredients

2 tbsp groundnut oil

2 red onions,
cut into thin wedges

175 g/6 oz red cabbage,
thinly shredded

225 g/8 oz pak choi

2 tbsp plum sauce

100 g/3½ oz roasted
cashew nuts, to garnish

Method

1 Heat the oil in a large preheated wok until it is really hot. Add the onion wedges to the wok and stir-fry for about 5 minutes, or until the onions are just beginning to brown.

2 Add the red cabbage and stir-fry for a further 5 minutes.

3 Add the pak choi leaves and stir-fry for about 2–3 minutes, or until the leaves have just wilted. Drizzle the plum sauce over the vegetables, toss together until well mixed and heat until the liquid is bubbling.

4 Garnish with the roasted cashew nuts and transfer to warmed serving bowls. Serve immediately.

★ Variation

For a more savoury flavour, replace the plum sauce with oyster sauce.

EGG NOODLES WITH TOFU & MUSHROOMS

Serves: 4   **Prep: 10–15 mins**   **Cook: 20 mins**

Ingredients

3 tbsp groundnut oil

2 dried red chillies

250 g/9 oz medium egg noodles

1 garlic clove, crushed

200 g/7 oz firm tofu, cut into 1-cm/½-inch cubes

200 g/7 oz oyster or chestnut mushrooms, sliced

2 tbsp lime juice

2 tbsp soy sauce

1 tsp brown sugar

fresh red chillies, to garnish

Method

1 Heat the oil in a wok and add the chillies. Heat gently for 10 minutes. Discard the fried chillies.

2 Cook the noodles in boiling water for 4 minutes, or according to the packet instructions. Drain.

3 Add the garlic and tofu to the wok and stir-fry on a high heat until golden. Remove with a slotted spoon and keep hot.

4 Add the mushrooms to the wok and stir-fry for 2–3 minutes to soften.

5 Stir in the lime juice, soy sauce and sugar.

6 Return the noodles and garlic tofu to the wok and toss to mix thoroughly.

7 Serve immediately, garnished with fresh chillies.

VEGETABLES

AUBERGINE STIR-FRY WITH HOT & SOUR SAUCE

Serves: 4   **Prep: 15–20 mins**   **Cook: 10–12 mins**

Ingredients

150 ml/5 fl oz vegetable stock

2 aubergines

6 tbsp groundnut oil

2 red peppers, deseeded and cut into matchstick strips

100 g/3½ oz canned water chestnuts, drained and sliced

6 spring onions, sliced

2 tsp finely chopped fresh ginger

1 large garlic clove, thinly sliced

1 green chilli, deseeded and finely chopped

1 tsp sesame seeds and thinly sliced spring onion tops, to garnish

Sauce

1½ tbsp soy sauce

1½ tbsp rice vinegar

2 tsp sugar

2 tsp cornflour, blended to a smooth paste with a little water

Method

1 First prepare the sauce. Combine the soy sauce, rice vinegar and sugar in a small bowl, stirring to dissolve the sugar. Mix in the cornflour paste and stir until smooth.

2 Heat the stock and set aside. Slice the aubergines in half lengthways. With the flat side facing down, slice each half lengthways into 1-cm/½-inch strips. Slice the wider strips lengthways in half again, then cut all the strips crossways into 4-cm/1½-inch pieces.

3 Heat a wok over a high heat and add 5 tablespoons of the oil. Add the aubergine and red pepper strips and stir-fry for 2–3 minutes until just beginning to colour. Remove from the wok and drain on kitchen paper. Heat the remaining tablespoon of oil over a high heat. Stir-fry the water chestnuts, spring onions, ginger, garlic and chilli for 1 minute.

4 Return the aubergine and red pepper to the wok. Reduce the heat to medium, and add the sauce and the stock. Stir-fry for 2–3 minutes until slightly thickened. Sprinkle with sesame seeds and sliced spring onion tops. Serve immediately.

SICHUAN MIXED VEGETABLES

Serves: 4   **Prep: 15 mins**   **Cook: 10 mins**

Ingredients

2 tbsp chilli oil

4 garlic cloves, crushed

5-cm/2-inch piece grated fresh ginger

250 g/9 oz carrots, cut into thin strips

1 red pepper, cut into thin strips

150 g/5½ oz shiitake mushrooms, sliced

150 g/5½ oz mangetout, halved diagonally

3 tbsp soy sauce

3 tbsp peanut butter

350 g/12 oz beansprouts

cooked rice, to serve

Method

1 Heat the chilli oil in a preheated wok and fry the garlic, ginger and carrots for 3 minutes. Add the pepper and stir-fry for another 2 minutes.

2 Add the mushrooms and mangetout and stir-fry for 1 minute.

3 In a small bowl, mix together the soy sauce and peanut butter until combined.

4 Using a wooden spoon, make a space in the centre of the stir-fried vegetables so that the base of the wok is visible. Pour in the sauce and bring to the boil, stirring all the time until it starts to thicken. Add the beansprouts and toss the vegetables to coat thoroughly with the sauce.

5 Transfer to a warmed serving dish and serve immediately with freshly cooked rice.

CABBAGE & WALNUT STIR-FRY

Serves: 4   **Prep: 15 mins**   **Cook: 12–13 mins**

Ingredients

4 tbsp groundnut oil

1 tbsp walnut oil

2 garlic cloves, crushed

350 g/12 oz white cabbage, thinly shredded

350 g/12 oz red cabbage, thinly shredded

8 spring onions, trimmed

225 g/8 oz firm tofu, cubed

2 tbsp lemon juice

100 g/3½ oz walnut halves

2 tsp Dijon mustard

salt and pepper

2 tsp poppy seeds, to garnish

Method

1 Heat the oils in a preheated wok. Add the garlic, white and red cabbage, spring onions and tofu and cook for 5 minutes, stirring.

2 Add the lemon juice, walnuts and mustard to the wok and stir to combine thoroughly.

3 Season the mixture to taste with salt and pepper and cook for a further 5 minutes, or until the cabbage is tender.

4 Transfer the stir-fry to a warmed serving bowl, garnish with poppy seeds and serve immediately.

ASIAN VEGETABLES WITH YELLOW BEAN SAUCE

Serves: 4

Prep: 15–20 mins, plus standing

Cook: 10 mins

Ingredients

1 aubergine

2 tbsp vegetable oil

3 garlic cloves, crushed

4 spring onions, chopped

1 small red pepper, deseeded and thinly sliced

4 baby corn, halved lengthways

115 g/4 oz mangetout

200 g/7 oz green pak choi, coarsely shredded

425 g/15 oz canned straw mushrooms, drained

115 g/4 oz fresh beansprouts

2 tbsp Chinese rice wine or dry sherry

2 tbsp yellow bean sauce

2 tbsp dark soy sauce

1 tsp chilli sauce

1 tsp sugar

150 ml/5 fl oz vegetable stock

1 tsp cornflour

2 tsp water

salt

Method

1 Cut the aubergine into 5-cm/2-inch-long thin sticks. Place in a colander, then sprinkle with a pinch of salt and let stand for 30 minutes. Rinse in cold water and dry thoroughly with kitchen paper.

2 Heat a wok over a medium–high heat and add the oil. Add the garlic, spring onions and pepper and stir-fry over a high heat for 1 minute. Stir in the aubergine pieces and stir-fry for a further minute, or until softened.

3 Stir in the baby corn and mangetout and stir-fry for 1 minute. Add the pak choi, mushrooms and beansprouts and stir-fry for 30 seconds.

4 Mix the rice wine, yellow bean sauce, soy sauce, chilli sauce and sugar together in a bowl, then add to the pan with the stock. Bring to the boil, stirring constantly.

5 Blend the cornflour with the water to form a smooth paste, then stir quickly into the pan and cook for a further minute. Serve immediately.

STIR-FRIED BUTTERNUT SQUASH

Serves: 2   **Prep: 25 mins**   **Cook: 20–30 mins**

Ingredients

1 butternut squash, weighing about 500 g/1 lb 2 oz

6 large shiitake mushrooms

5 tbsp rapeseed oil

½ tsp white peppercorns, crushed

½ tsp coriander seeds, crushed

2 large garlic cloves, thinly sliced

finely grated zest of ½ lemon

½ tbsp rice vinegar

4 tbsp chicken or vegetable stock

2 good handfuls of baby spinach, stalks removed

sea salt flakes

chopped fresh coriander, to garnish

Method

1 Cut the squash in two crossways and remove the skin. Quarter the rounded part and remove the seeds and fibres. Slice lengthways into thin segments. Slice the neck in half lengthways, then crossways into thin semicircles. Discard the stalks from the mushrooms, and thinly slice the caps.

2 Heat a wok over a medium–high heat, then add the oil. Add half the crushed peppercorns and coriander seeds. Stir for a few seconds, then add the squash in small batches. Fry for 5–7 minutes, turning with tongs, until lightly browned and just tender. Sprinkle with sea salt flakes. Using a slotted spoon, transfer to a large sieve set over a bowl.

3 Add the mushrooms to the wok and fry for 4–5 minutes, using some of the oil drained from the squash. Add the garlic and lemon zest, and fry for another minute. Sprinkle with sea salt flakes and the remaining coriander seeds and peppercorns. Add to the squash.

4 Pour any oil drained from the vegetables into the wok. Stir in the vinegar and stock, and simmer for a few seconds until slightly reduced.

5 Arrange the spinach on warmed plates, pile the vegetables on top, then pour over the wok juices. Garnish with coriander and serve immediately.

VEGETABLES

CAULIFLOWER & BEANS WITH CASHEW NUTS

Serves: 2 **Prep: 10–15 mins** **Cook: 10–14 mins**

Ingredients

2 tbsp vegetable or groundnut oil

1 tbsp chilli oil

1 onion, chopped

2 garlic cloves, chopped

2 tbsp red curry paste

1 small cauliflower, cut into florets

175 g/6 oz runner beans, cut into 7.5-cm/3-inch lengths

150 ml/5 fl oz vegetable stock

2 tbsp Thai soy sauce

50 g/1¾ oz toasted cashew nuts, to garnish

Method

1 In a preheated wok, heat the oils, then add the onion and garlic and stir-fry until soft. Add the curry paste and stir-fry for 1–2 minutes.

2 Add the cauliflower and beans and stir-fry for 3–4 minutes, until soft. Pour in the stock and soy sauce and simmer for 1–2 minutes. Serve immediately, garnished with the cashew nuts.

VEGETABLES

BROCCOLI & MANGETOUT STIR-FRY

Serves: 4　　　**Prep: 10–15 mins**　　　**Cook: 7 mins**

Ingredients

2 tbsp vegetable or groundnut oil

dash of sesame oil

1 garlic clove, finely chopped

225 g/8 oz small head of broccoli florets

115 g/4 oz mangetout, trimmed

225 g/8 oz Chinese leaves, chopped into 1-cm/½-inch slices

5–6 spring onions, finely chopped

½ tsp salt

2 tbsp light soy sauce

1 tbsp Shaoxing rice wine

1 tsp sesame seeds, lightly toasted, to garnish

Method

1 In a preheated wok, heat the oils, then add the garlic and stir-fry vigorously. Add all the vegetables and salt and stir-fry over high heat, tossing rapidly, for about 3 minutes.

2 Pour in the light soy sauce and rice wine, and cook for a further 2 minutes. Garnish with the sesame seeds and serve immediately.

VEGETABLES

TOFU STIR-FRY

Serves: 4 **Prep: 10–15 mins** **Cook: 10–15 mins**

Ingredients

2 tbsp sunflower oil

350 g/12 oz firm tofu, cubed

225 g/8 oz pak choi, roughly chopped

1 garlic clove, chopped

4 tbsp sweet chilli sauce

2 tbsp light soy sauce

Method

1 Heat a wok over a high heat, then add 1 tablespoon of the oil. Add the tofu to the wok in batches and stir-fry for 2–3 minutes, until golden. Remove and set aside.

2 Add the pak choi to the wok and stir-fry for a few seconds, until tender and wilted. Remove and set aside.

3 Heat the remaining oil in the wok, then add the garlic and stir-fry for 30 seconds.

4 Stir in the chilli sauce and soy sauce and bring to the boil. Return the tofu and pak choi to the wok and toss gently until coated in the sauce. Serve immediately.

THAI NOODLE SALAD

Serves: 4

Prep: 15 mins,
plus soaking

Cook: 5 mins

Ingredients

200 g/7 oz fine rice noodles

2 tbsp groundnut oil

1 red onion, thinly sliced

2 carrots, cut into matchsticks

125 g/4½ oz baby corn, halved lengthways

1 garlic clove, crushed

150 g/5½ oz beansprouts

2 tbsp fish sauce

juice of ½ lime

1 tsp caster sugar

½ tsp dried chilli flakes

4 tbsp coriander, chopped

4 spring onions, thinly sliced

40 g/1½ oz toasted peanuts

lime wedges, to serve

Method

1 Soak the noodles in hot water for 10 minutes, or according to the packet instructions. Drain well and set aside.

2 Heat the oil in a wok and stir-fry the onion for 1 minute. Add the carrots and baby corn and stir-fry for 2 minutes. Stir in the garlic then remove from the heat.

3 Stir in the beansprouts, then tip into a bowl and add the noodles, tossing to mix evenly.

4 Mix together the fish sauce, lime juice, caster sugar, chillies and half the coriander.

5 Spoon into serving bowls, then sprinkle with spring onions, peanuts and the remaining coriander. Serve hot, with lime wedges.

MUSHROOMS & FRENCH BEANS WITH LEMON & CORIANDER

Serves: 2　　　　**Prep: 15 mins**　　　　**Cook: 10 mins**

Ingredients

450 g/1 lb mixed small mushrooms such as cremini, enoki and buna shimeji

6 tbsp rapeseed oil

1 tsp coriander seeds, crushed

1 fresh bay leaf

175 g/6 oz French beans

1 large garlic clove, thinly sliced

3 tbsp lemon juice

2 tsp soy sauce

2 tbsp chopped coriander

2 tsp sesame oil

2 tsp sesame seeds

salt and pepper

Method

1　Rinse the mushrooms and dry with kitchen paper. If using clumping mushrooms, such as enoki and buna shimeji, slice off the root and separate the clump. Slice cremini mushrooms in half.

2　Heat a wok over a medium–high heat and add the oil. Add the coriander seeds and bay leaf, and fry for a few seconds to flavour the oil. Add the mushrooms and beans, and stir-fry for 5 minutes.

3　Stir in the garlic, lemon juice and soy sauce. Season with salt and pepper, and stir-fry for 2 minutes. Sprinkle with the coriander, sesame oil and seeds, and fry for a few seconds. Remove the bay leaf and serve immediately.

★ Variation

For a different flavour stir in black bean sauce at step 3.

INDEX